Life Writing:
A Guide to
Family Journals
and
Personal Memoirs

Life Writing:
A Guide to
Family Journals
and
Personal Memoirs

William J. Hofmann

St. Martin's Press   New York

Library of Congress Cataloging in Publication Data
Hofmann, William J.
Life writing, a guide to family journals &
personal memoirs.

1. Genealogy—Handbooks, manuals, etc. I. Title.
CS16.H62   929'.1   81-21529
ISBN 0-312-48507-7   AACR2

To Ellen,
source of my best memoirs

For Kathlyn, Karen, Kirsten, Romy, and Margo,
sources of things to come

Contents

I am the family face;
Flesh perishes, I live on,
Projecting trait and trace
Through time to times anon,
And leaping from place to place
Over oblivion.
—Thomas Hardy, "Heredity"
Moments of Vision, (1917)

Introduction

Who should write the family history?

The answer is the family—the young, the middle-aged, the elderly—all should write. A young woman in one of my college classes wrote about her experience in childbirth with her firstborn. She wrote of her feelings, her fears, and her hopes; she wrote about the husband at her side, and she wrote about her child in its first moments of life. When I returned her story, I wrote on it, "Save this as a record of a special moment. You and your child will enjoy reading this in the years to come."

Her response was, "I will. I think it's the best thing I've ever written. I showed it to my mother, and she wants a copy. But I told her I wouldn't give it to her, not until she wrote something about what it was like when I was born."

In another class I asked students to write about a special day in their lives. A young man turned in a three-page composition about a day he had spent with his father. The young man was fourteen at the time, and his father, who drove a delivery truck, had said, "Hey, son, want to make my rounds with me today?"

The son wrote that it was on that day he saw his father

fully for the first time. He saw him on the job and met the foreman and his father's fellow workers. He saw his father dealing with the customers on his route, saw and heard how other people respected his father, talked with his father between deliveries and discovered a wisdom and warmth that gave a new dimension to their relationship.

Everyone has something of value to say about his or her family experience. In workshops I've had people from thirty-nine to ninety-three writing about everything from homesteading to troop trains, from sleeping porches to assassinations.

What is such writing? Is it family history? Is it personal memoir? Is it biographical sketch? Is it just "storytelling"? It doesn't matter what you call it, but it *matters!* It's important to the writer and it's important to the other members of the family, now and in the future.

My advice to the young man was to give what he had written to his father on Father's Day. The father will never receive a better gift, and I know the young man will himself grow old still cherishing the original experience and the fact that he shared his impressions with his dad. And *because* he has written it, his child and his grandchild will share in it also.

It's that kind of sharing that this book is all about.

Prewriting

i Putting Your Fears to Rest

> Writing is about as hard or as easy as gardening
> or golf, as carpentry or cooking.

In my experience as a teacher, I found many students, both young and old, who were fearful of writing. The responsibility overwhelmed them. They were terrified at the prospect of having to say something SIGNIFICANT! Imagine what would happen if you said to yourself, "I can't get out of bed today unless I'm going to do something significant." Or, "I can't speak a word unless I say something significant." We would all be horizontal mutes staring at the ceiling if we had to live by such standards.

Others view writing as a "divine gift," an act of genius and inspiration, something few are born with. There's more fiction than fact in that notion. Writing is a task, a chore, a craft, an art. You can put as much or as little into it as you put into any other task or craft. It is no more difficult than you choose to make it.

Put your writing in perspective: Compare it to cooking. The meal was prepared in a matter of hours; it was enjoyed by yourself and a handful of friends and family. You were satisfied enough with that small "audience." You could take some pride in your effort; you nourished them and gave them pleasure. You didn't worry about what the world would think of you and your meal—so don't worry about what the world will think of you and your writing. Your memoirs and family history are for the pleasure and nourishment of family and friends. For you and for them, your writing has value. Be content with that.

Writing need not be any more complicated than cooking or carpentry or gardening. Some people may do it better than others, but writing isn't any harder than the multitude of other human tasks you have already performed in your lifetime. That's our first premise for this chapter: *Writing is no more complicated than most other life skills.*

Let's consider a few examples. Did you ever take a snapshot with your camera? Did you ever watch others snapping pictures right and left? People who take pictures rarely ask themselves, "Is this going to be significant?" They take for granted that a face or an occasion should be preserved.

Family albums are full of photographs that are blurred, faded, awkwardly posed, or unnatural. But we love those pictures. We cherish those frail and faulty images, because they are all we have of lost moments. We are glad somebody took the time to snap a picture. When we look at them, we rarely say, "I wish it were a more artistic photograph." We more often say, "I wish there were more pictures of . . ."

Well, there are more pictures. Thousands of them. They are in your memory, and they can be developed on paper. You can do things with your simple, basic writing that can never be done with a camera. In the writing of your memoirs and family history, you can do things that poor, mute, frozen photographs can never do. For every

4

moment a camera is ready, there are ten thousand moments only the mind can record and only words can reveal.

Seeing Your Writing for What It Is

Family albums have been popular for a long time. They represent one kind of family history. Recently more formal genealogy has become popular; researching the family tree back four or five or six generations has become another way of discovering who we are and where we came from. When you write your memoirs or family history, you are not competing with photographic albums or genealogies; you are providing a third type of information —information that cannot be had in any other way.

The genealogy or family tree reaches back in time, before your life, outlining names and dates. Photographs represent a few hundred visual seconds, brief fragments. Neither genealogy nor photograph is alive the way your narratives and sketches will be alive. Neither is capable of the range and detail and personality that your writing can provide. One is not a substitute for the other. No one can ever research your mind or photograph what it knows and remembers. Only you can reveal it through speech and writing. Speech is transient; writing is permanent.

Yes, writing is permanent, if you can ever get it down on paper in the first place. So cast off any doubts and fears. You can't fail if you write; silence is the only absolute failure. Each sentence is a small success.

Writing As a Regular Routine

Our first premise is that *writing is no more complicated than most other life skills.* It takes a little time; it takes a little effort. But a room never got painted by thinking about it, and potatoes never got peeled by a good intention. You have to put your hands to the task. You have to put words on paper.

Like most tasks, writing is not accomplished in a sudden spasm of activity or in a flash of insight. Photographs may be made that way; and ideas may be born that way; but paragraphs and pages are made like the day: minute by minute, hour by hour, word by word, with the rising and setting of the sun.

Think of writing like gardening or raising chickens or building a boat or playing a game of golf. It involves time, a variety of different acts focused on a clear objective, and some trial and error. Regular practice makes you better at it, but the goal is as easy or as hard as you choose to make it.

And there are really two kinds of objectives: the immediate and the long range. In gardening the near objective for the day may be to break up the soil; the distant objective, months down the line, is harvesting pumpkins. So it is with writing—there is something to be done now and something to be harvested in the future, with a lot of hoeing and weeding in between.

Expect to write only three or four pages of rough copy per day. Be content if you get only one or two. Write every day. Don't save it up or say, "I'll spend all Saturday on it." Work at it one board at a time, one row at a time, one shovelful at a time, one stitch at a time. Writing takes shape the way anything else does, a little at a time.

Pick a specific time of day in which to write. For example, my grandmother did her gardening between 8:30 and 10:00 in the morning, when it was cool, after breakfast was done and lunch not yet started. Her sewing rarely came out of the basket before afternoon or evening. My grandfather had his routines when he stoked the furnace in winter or trimmed the hedges in summer.

Neither of them got up in the mornings and asked, "Should I work today?" There was only the quiet recognition, "It is time now." The natural rhythm and routine of their lives carried them forward.

So with your writing. Have a time for it. Let it become a part of your routine, a part of the natural rhythm of your life, something you do every day. Go to your task with the understanding that "It is time now for me to write."

And accept the fact that it is a task—sometimes tedious, sometimes pleasant, sometimes gratifying. Like many tasks, writing itself will not get easier, but it may get better, and gradually you will not fight yourself or the material so much. You will not ask, "Should I?" or "Can I?" or "Is it worth it?" or "What will my friends think?" You will do it as well as you can. And the more you write, the more you will learn about writing, about your subjects, and about yourself.

In all this there is something of the biblical sweat of the brow and a bit of casting of bread upon the waters. Give yourself to the task and don't question your talents or motives. Your labors will reward you.

That brings us to our second premise: *Accept the fact that the writing will take time and effort; it will fill many hours and days. Tomorrow and for years to come, as it reaches your audience, it will fill minds and nourish imaginations. In writing, your labor bears fruit for generations.*

ii You, Your Message, Your Audience

> Think plain. Think simple. Think small. Good
> writing can come from plain people saying simple
> things.

You have not read many pieces like those you should be
writing. You haven't seen "memoirs" and "family history" in most magazines and newspapers. Therefore, you
haven't many models with which to compare your writing. The reason for this is that the type of writing we are
talking about usually does not have commercial potential
and therefore is not publishable. Take the following example:

Our Wellhouse
The wellhouse was pantry, root cellar and ice box,
all in one. It was a log shed about nine feet long and
six feet wide with a sod roof and no windows, so the
heat of the sun never got in. The floor was packed
dirt, and the interior was cool, dark, and smelled of
the earth.

The well was in one corner. It was only about twelve or fifteen feet deep, the upper six feet being lined with wooden boards to prevent cave-in. A board frame and hinged cover fit tightly over the top to keep stray mice out. There was no windlass for the rope and bucket. We had to haul the water up hand over hand.

On the down-hill side of the wellhouse was a shallow pit dug next to the wall, and in that we kept things like butter and milk and the like which had to be chilled. Everything in the pit was in jars and covered over with burlap sacks that had been wetted down with water from the well. On even the hottest days the milk came out cool and fresh.

Along the interior walls were shelves which . . .

Normally that would not be considered "publishable" material, but that's as good as your writing need ever be. What you are writing about yourself and the family is probably not salable, and it is not meant for publication by a commercial firm to be read by a mass audience. Our assumption for this chapter and for the entire book is: *You are a normal person with a modest story for a small audience.*

And that makes a world of difference! Most of the advice on what to write about and how to write is based on the assumption that the writer is striving for publication. Most writing guidelines assume a mass audience in the thousands or millions. But you and I are talking about writing for a few dozen friends and relatives—and some other people who haven't been born yet.

How does that change the writing? In many ways. It means you can relax. Your small audience is highly sympathetic and personally interested in your material. You don't have to worry about selling them anything. It's not costing them; you are giving them something they will value more and more as time goes on. Your writing will be a family treasury of facts and images, not a best-seller.

You don't have to pander to popular taste in certain topics. Your information is perennially in fashion. Instead of losing value and interest, your information increases in value and interest with the passing years. Few writers can say that.

You don't have to worry about being highly dramatic, intriguing, suspenseful, funny, entertaining, or even grammatically correct. Such things may be important for commercial writers competing in the mass market, but you are writing something no more difficult than a letter to a friend or a relative. If you and your material can from time to time be funny, dramatic, or entertaining, that's fine. But it's not a constant necessity. Don't worry about it. Your material will be valued more for its content than for its form.

On the other hand, if you insist on writing a bestseller, you are on your own. The advice and instructions here aim at the more modest goal of simple, personal topics written in casual, readable prose.

Define Your Audience

If you aren't writing for a mass audience, whom are you writing for? You need to know. You need to think about that audience. You probably have some idea already, but take a few minutes now to make a tentative list of those persons or families to whom you will give copies of your memoirs or family history. It will be a preliminary working list; you can add to it or subtract from it as you go along. Just keep it simple.

My suggestion for your "audience list" would be your immediate family members and very close friends. For example, my list would include my sister's family, which consists of her, her husband, and her two boys. Her family would receive one copy of my writing. My wife's brother and his family would receive another copy. I would want one copy for each of my five daughters.

And I would want the original and a copy for my use. If someone wanted to borrow my memoirs for a while, I'd give that person the loaner copy. I'd keep the original clean and safely filed away in the event that I wanted to run some additional copies later on. The method of copying is discussed in Chapter XII on reproduction. Here we are concerned only with defining the audience to whom we will distribute the first copies.

My list starts to look like this:

my sister's family	1 copy
my wife's brother and family	1 copy
my daughters and their families	
Kathlyn	1 copy
Karen	1 copy
Kirsten	1 copy
Romy	1 copy
Margo	1 copy
personal copies—original plus	1 copy

And I would probably add to that basic family list:

my wife's parents	1 copy

Those are the obvious and easy ones. I come from a small family, and I'm up to nine copies for an audience of twenty or so.

I have a maternal aunt, widowed, and a paternal uncle. I would probably consult them as I wrote my memoirs, and I would feel obligated to give them copies.

Aunt Marion	1 copy
Uncle Howard	1 copy

Eleven copies—that's where I would stop, at least for now.

If you come from a large family or have a large family, your list may call for twenty or thirty copies. You make the decision on that. My advice is to take ten minutes now and jot down your preliminary list. Give your immediate audience names and faces.

Your Annual Installment

Give your audience something to read within the next year, if not sooner. Give them a yearly installment on the family history or, better still, a family magazine. There are advantages to handing out copy on a regular and frequent basis rather than trying to save everything for one massive lump of memoir:

1. A regular installment will help you keep in mind that you should be writing plain and simple pieces —short pieces, not 60,000-word autobiographies— brief stories about how you got your first job, what the old wellhouse looked like, a description of your fourth-grade Christmas party, or your first trip away from home. The regular installment implies a series of short pieces that are part of the larger mosaic of family life.
2. A regular installment will give you a deadline. It will enhance your self-discipline if you make a commitment to write something on a regular basis and deliver it on schedule.
3. You will get more frequent feedback and encouragement. You won't have to write for years, wondering if the family will appreciate your efforts.
4. You might inspire some volunteers to pitch in, either with typing or artwork or reproduction. You might get some others to begin writing, also.

5. You will avoid massive costs for one-time reproduction and binding of a manuscript that, in the
   end, may run to several hundred pages.
6. Nothing is final. After an annual edition is out, you
   still have the option to expand or edit the material
   later on or to recombine the short pieces according
   to theme or time or place. You can experiment one
   year, try a different approach or group of subjects
   the next year, until you arrive at exactly what you
   want.

I like the idea of an annual Christmas issue or Hanuk-
kah volume or birthday magazine. Your memoirs and
family history make an excellent gift with a nice personal
touch and are of very special interest to your select audience. Moreover, your writing gift will go on giving for
years, even generations. (If nothing else, writing the family history should simplify your Christmas shopping.)

While your readership list is fresh in front of you, go
ahead and write down your first distribution date. You are
going to write a few short pieces, reproduce them, and
deliver the copies to your family audience on . . . ?

The Writing Program

If you've got that distribution list and your first "publication" date, you've already completed the first two steps
in the writing program. Let's take a look at the program
that awaits you:

1. You identify your audience and list the names of
   relatives and friends who will receive copies of
   your writing.
2. You commit yourself to a deadline. You are going
   to give the family the first installment of your
   work on a set date.

3. You make a list of topics and stories, things you'd like to write about. That list will grow and change over the months and years.

4. You develop a daily routine of writing, trying to turn out two or three or four pages of rough copy a day.

5. The first simple topic in rough-draft form takes shape. Maybe you write about the wild fawn, Bucky, that you fed and raised.

6. You write the second short piece, the story that you've told so often in the past about you and your sister spending the night alone.

7. You write twelve or fourteen pages describing the family's readjustment to life in a new community.

8. You write a description and biographical sketch dealing with Uncle Fred and the small business he ran.

9. You write a short comic piece about your brother the summer he got into the poison ivy.

10. *You revise each of the preceding until it meets your reasonable expectations.*

11. You prepare the final draft of each piece, adding any photographs or artwork to go along with it.

12. You reproduce, collate, bind, and distribute the first annual installment of your family history.

And you start again, preparing next year's installment. Maybe you'll do a few things a little differently, but the basic routine will be there. You will find the task less formidable and more rewarding with each piece you write.

Look again at the writing program. It calls for only five incidents or topics, and those pieces don't necessarily follow any particular order. Their unity is provided by your personality and the fact that they all have something to do with the loose concept of "family." Each short incident will be organized and unified and developed in its own right, but the package of five incidents is fairly loose.

And that's the way I recommend you begin writing your family history: *Short, simple selections that will stand alone and can be loosely grouped together.* That way you don't have to conceive and follow some master plan before you start to write. You don't have to bury yourself in years of research. You are free to range over a variety of topics and to go immediately to those things you know and would like to write about.

Plain, simple, small. Think in terms of a rowboat, not an ocean liner; of dinner for a few friends, not a banquet for thousands; of cutting and sewing a dress, not costuming the cast for the Metropolitan Opera's production of *Aïda.*

And if you are ready to start on your first short piece now, then do so. Go ahead and write your first rough draft, because the best advice about writing applies to revision rather than the first draft. Dive in.

If, however, you're not sure where to start, read on into the next chapter, which discusses topics for your short pieces.

iii A Multitude of Topics

> The goal here is to free up the mind, to let the ideas flow, and to discover that we know many things on which to write.

"What should I write about?"

"Where should I start?"

"What should I say?"

All are valid questions, but they do not have to be answered all at once. Question number one asks about topics, number two about organization, and number three about development. In this chapter we deal only with the question on topics: What should you write about?

The answer here, as in the previous chapter, is to write about something simple, easy, and familiar. Write about the people, places, objects, events, and thoughts that have been part of your life. Plain, simple, familiar topics.

This business of what to write about—the choice of topics—is one of the worst hang-ups in all writing. But for the writer of memoirs and family history, this problem can be solved quickly and permanently. It's a bit like looking in your closet in the morning and saying, "What shall I wear?" Or opening the refrigerator and saying, "What shall I cook for dinner?" As long as you agree not to go naked and not to starve, you'll find something to wear and to eat. There are lots of choices, but you have to make a choice.

Goals, Definition, and Principles

There are four things this chapter can do for you:

1. It can show you that there is a multitude of topics to write about and that you possess the knowledge to write about them.
2. It can give you a beginning list of topics and ideas for your writing.
3. It can suggest a few approaches and techniques to help you build your future list.
4. It can start you on your actual writing.

Definitions aren't terribly important here, but to clear up any confusion, let's say that *subjects* are broad areas of discussion; that *topics* are limited, tightly focused ideas; and that *themes* are subtle, either tonal qualities or underlying interpretations that may be suggestive rather than openly stated. Thus a *subject*, such as my mother, may suggest dozens of possible *topics*, each one generating a separate essay or composition. The same *theme*—say, her dignity under stress—might be suggested in several of the topics.

When we speak of topics, we are talking about a narrow, limited, tightly focused and contained idea. Subjects or broad topics are difficult to control and develop, and they take a long time to write. You should write something simple that can be completed within a few days or weeks. Then we will take those simple units and build our greater structure.

Topics must be not only narrow and limited, they must be specific and concrete, not general and abstract. We had an abstract poke its head in here recently—it was called Dignity Under Stress. (Abstractions almost cry out for capital letters: Love, Honor, Equality, Justice, Nobility, etc.) Watch out for abstractions! They may stand for significant qualities, but they produce some of the worst writing in the world. Let the important qualities that abstractions stand for emerge as *themes,* subtle and unspoken. Write about things you can see, hear, taste, touch, and smell.

For example, in the following piece by Carl Cleveland of Mercer Island, Washington, you will find him writing about his grandfather's pocketknife.

Granddad's Jackknife
by Carl M. Cleveland, Copyright 1977

Man, for all his ingenuity, has never perfected a tool of greater simplicity and at the same time utility and versatility than Granddad's jackknife.

It seems to me a mark of decadence that few men today carry a jackknife, or for that matter, a knife of any kind. Granddad would have felt but half dressed without his knife in his pocket.

With its plain bone handle, the knife encompassed only two blades and an awl-punch. Very likely it would be illegal today for I believe the larger of the two blades was more than four inches long.

Granddad kept the blades whetted to razor sharpness, honing them first on a whetstone—which was lubricated with a judicious application of saliva.

The final edge was achieved by stropping on Granddad's razor strap. Occasionally he would "touch it up" on the palm of his hand. His straight razor and his jackknife were of equal sharpness. While I never saw him do it, I'm quite sure Granddad could have carried out his boast that he could shave with his knife.

I have fond memories of the knife because of the many ways in which I shared in its versatility. With the needle-like point of the small blade, Granddad would remove slivers from finger or foot.

When I suffered cuts, or stepped on a nail, Granddad would make a slash in the balsam tree in the front yard. Then, with the flat of a blade, he would remove the oozing pitch and apply it to the wound. The pitch served to stop bleeding, seal the wound, and it must have had a medicinal quality for the cuts and bruises invariably healed smoothly.

Down in the garden, beyond the Wealthy apple tree and close to Granddad's ginseng lath house, was a melon patch. Granddad would smell out a ripe "mush-melon," cut it from the vine, flip out the seeds and then slice it into new-moon-shaped crescents. If you haven't eaten melon 20 seconds from the vine, you really don't know what a melon is.

To explain the ginseng—its root is highly prized by the Chinese who make extensive use of it in their medicinal herbs. Granddad raised it commercially. It and maple syrup were the two cash crops of the farm.

In the spring Granddad would cut willow branches and making deft incisions with the trusty knife, would slip off the bark, shape the bare wood, replace the slipped bark and—presto—we had a whistle.

Also in the spring Granddad would cut out strips of bark from the "slippery elm" tree. Chewed, it induced a prodigious flow of saliva and we would play we were chewing tobacco.

If old Bess got a bit lazy while pulling the cultivator through the rows of corn, out would come the knife, Granddad would cut a switch and a few taps with it would restore Bess' interest in her work.

Once one of the milk cows, in her greediness, swallowed a potato whole. Choking badly, she was in real distress. With the razor-sharp blade of his knife

Granddad performed a tracheotomy, removed the potato, sewed up the wound and covered it with balsam pitch. The cow suffered no ill effects, except that she disdained potatoes in any form thereafter.

Each fall in hunting season Granddad "got his deer." The antlered animal would be suspended from a rafter in the wood shed and out would come the jackknife. With it Granddad would skin the carcass and then with knife and saw, cut it into steaks, and roasts.

Then, when one of the steaks reached the table, there again was Granddad's knife—he wouldn't trust table wear to cut his meat. The meal finished, Granddad would select a sliver of pine and from it fashion a toothpick for himself.

When old Bess' harness needed mending, Granddad would cut and trim the leather straps with the faithful knife and make the necessary buckle holes with the awl which partnered the two blades.

By the deftness of his touch Granddad could pare an entire apple in one long coiled peeling, which we converted into necklaces. Or he might halve a Wealthy—that apple of ambrosial taste and pink-stripped flesh—giving one part to me and the other to my cousin Esther.

On cold winter evenings, snug as we were around the base heater, Granddad would take kindling from the woodbox and whittle shavings on each stick. They were to be used in the morning to start the fire.

Surplus milk from the farm was taken to the cheese factory. The factory always had a wheel of cheese sitting on the counter for sampling by its customers. With the always-present knife Granddad would cut small wedges of cheese for each of us. At the same time the cheesemaker would be filling our milk cans with whey for the pigs.

Finally, while Grandma visited her relatives, Granddad would join the men who sat on benches in front of Pankratz' saloon at "The Corners." Like the others, he would pick up a bit of wood and start whittling. Many philosophical and political discussions took place while the men were thus engaged.

It seems to me a basic element missing from politics today is whittling.

Maybe if more men carried jackknives and knew how to use them our elections might be more meaningful.

The whole premise of this chapter is echoed in that short piece. The topic is narrow and specific—not any pocketknife, but Granddad's pocketknife. Mr. Cleveland saw it, touched it, and probably tasted its metallic tinge on the apple slice—that's good sensory detail. But what kind of man was Granddad? What words would you use to characterize him? Was he, too, versatile, capable, quick, gentle, clever, honest, reliable, loving? We have a *feel* for the grandfather that is more real and meaningful because Carl Cleveland avoided those abstractions and let us see the grandfather in action through the device of the jackknife.

You don't have to set out to write beautiful, rich, subtle pieces. You write about the familiar, well-remembered, simple topics, and the beauty, richness, and humanity will emerge, even as it does here.

As a first step, you should begin right now making a list of possible topics. Take a sheet of paper and list topics and ideas that occur to you as you are reading this chapter. Keep adding to that list every day. Don't worry about the order or the sequence of the ideas. Soon you'll need a writing tablet or notebook to keep the growing list of topics. You don't have to write on all of them, but there won't be any shortage of ideas.

Triggering the Mind

Your mind is so full of information and ideas about yourself, your experiences, your family and friends, and all the things you've seen and done, it's not that you don't have anything to write about, it's that you have trouble releasing or triggering that stored potential. A single word, a picture, a sound, an odor, another idea is capable of triggering memories.

Here's a quick example:

animals . . .

pets . . .

insects . . .

List three or four topics—narrow, simple, specific ideas—relating to "insects." Include anything in your experience or in the experience of any member of your family.

Lightning bugs? Does that ring a bell? Does that trigger any memories? I could write a short piece about how we kids collected lightning bugs in fruit jars in the quiet summer evenings in southern Illinois.

Cicadas?

Bees? I had an uncle who kept bees. Writing about his beehives and the way he "worked" them would let me say a lot about him.

Termites?

Roaches? . . . as fish bait?

Ant lions?

June bugs, tumble bugs, and so on . . . ?

Alkali bees? I wrote a piece once about a neighboring farmer who imported alkali bees to fertilize his alfalfa.

Moths? A woman in one of my workshops wrote an interesting profile of life on a barren north-Texas farm. One of the things they did there was hang old garments on a line outside the window at night. Moths drawn by the light of the coal-oil lamp would settle finally in the folds of the garments. The next morning they would take the garments and shake them over the chicken pen, and the chickens would eat the moths.

When I was a kid in Texas, we caught grasshoppers for the same purpose.

Butterflies? Lots of possibilities there.

Beetles?

Earwigs?

Wasps, hornets, yellow jackets, mud dobbers?

Mosquitoes? (You must be able to recall something related to mosquitoes.)

Fleas? Ticks?

Sow bugs, pill bugs?

Mealworms?

Ants? If that doesn't do it, nothing will. The point is this: We are not writing a scientific treatise about a particular insect. We are looking for associations, certain memories that might spring to life when one or more of these insect names triggers a certain idea or memory. You will write about the memory; the insect will only be part of it.

Look for the topics. They are there, and you will find drama in a farmer struggling to protect his crops from some ravaging insect; you will also find the reasons for some of the lines in his face. Or recount the wild, stumbling pursuit of fireflies and find what gave joy to youth. It's worth a few hundred words, and it's a good place to start your topic list.

Breaking the Broad Subject Area into Workable Topics

Let's take a broad subject area about how people amuse themselves. Head your list: Amusements, Games, and Hobbies.

Start listing:

hide 'n' seek	movies	church socials
blind-man's bluff	home movies	school picnics
tag	Saturday matinees	lodge picnics
jump rope	plays	family reunions
marbles	magic shows	
Hula-Hoops	dance recitals	

If one word here or on your own list causes you to think, "I remember the time . . ." or "I'll never forget when . . ." then a specific memory has been triggered. Chances are that will make a good topic to write about. Add a word or two to your list to remind you again what that specific event was about. Then go on with your list.

Here is what my slightly expanded list on this subject area might look like, especially if I only thought of my childhood:

1. ring toss (at the county fair; caused me to be drummed out of the Boy Scouts)
2. swinging on the wild grape vines
3. toy soldiers
    a. the lead ones I cast (and taking lead from old church windows to do it with)
    b. the flat tin ones
4. reading
    a. Big Little Books
    b. comic books
    c. browsing through Grandma's bookcase
5. my BB gun
6. battles with
    a. rubber guns
    b. pokeberries

    c.   black walnuts
    d.   snowballs

As I look back over that list, I see a separate topic in each item. Under 6 a, rubber guns, I'd have to explain what rubber guns were. (We made them with big rubber bands cut from old inner tubes. The guns shot those big rubber bands thirty or forty feet. Up close, they could deliver a real sting.) I'd have to assume that my grandchildren will probably never play with such toys, because inner tubes, especially those with much stretch, are on their way out. I'd be telling about how the guns were made, where we got the inner tubes, how we played at war, and finally how the guns "escalated" in size and power until our parents made us stop. My guess is that topic is worth seven or eight pages.

Take a minute to work through your own list. Jot down anything that comes to mind; you can always reject it later, but get the fleeting thought on paper now.

Why am I talking about rubber guns and toy soldiers? Well, because the objects come easily to mind, and because they will tell my readers about the games children played in my community. But above all, these simple topics and incidents *show* my readers what my childhood consisted of. Those topics will reveal me and the kind of child I was. That's what the personal memoir is all about.

Similarly, if I talk about the games my sister and I played, I come very quickly to one summer afternoon when she and her friend and I went to a movie matinee. The film was about forest firefighters, and we got caught up in the fantasy of the film. When we came home, we decided to play "firefighters." My sister would set small grass fires, and the friend and I would put them out. Without going into more detail here, let me say we almost burned the dairy down that day. My sister hid under the bed, and I had to talk her out after the fire engines left.

Now that I think of it, movies and books provided us

with inspiration for games of piracy, cowboys and Indians, nurse and doctor. The reader of such stories would learn a lot about the relationship between my sister and me as we were growing up. Given a chance, people and their personalities will emerge from what you write.

If you want to write about a brother or a sister, a topic based on toys or games would be one way to begin. If you want to write about your child, think of a game or toy or pastime out of his or her youth. For my daughter Kathlyn, I'd do a little piece about the swing I hung in the doorway when she was just a year old. It was the first time she'd been in a swing, and she had to take turns with her twin sister, Karen. Karen got tired of the swing and went off to other things. Kathlyn, like a pendulum, sat there chanting "lidabit more, lidabit more, peas. Lidabit more." Such brief vignettes are exactly the sort of thing that should be written up in a baby book or child diary. A collection of them could be assembled into a single childhood sketch.

In writing about yourself and your brothers and sisters, or about your children or your parents and aunts and uncles, look for comparison and contrast. I've suggested that daughter Karen contrasted with daughter Kathlyn about the swing. In later years it was daughter Romy who was most like Kathlyn, delighted with swinging for hours. Daughter Margo became terrified of swinging about the time she first started to walk—I could do a whole piece on swings, but mostly it would pull together an image of my several daughters. The topic grows out of the mental process of comparing and contrasting.

Clothing

For another subject area try clothing. Your favorite shoes, boots, dress, hat, pants, coats—or your sister's or mother's or grandfather's. Think of costumes, work clothes, dress clothes.

Make out your list, and then I'll tell you about mine. Ready? My first tuxedo. I grew up in a small town where only bankers and doctors had tuxedos, and most of those were old ones. For the high-school homecoming the boys who were class officers were to wear the dozen or so borrowed black-tie and white-tie outfits that could be scrounged from the community. As master of ceremonies, I got one of the better suits but had to wear shoes three sizes too big. That interfered with my dancing. But it was the freshmen officers, low men in the picking order, who wore the moth-eaten, undersize, Civil War models.

Some more topics on my list:

Chaps: I remember a rodeo in Wilson, Wyoming, where a city-slicker friend of mine thought chaps made him a cowboy.
Sunday clothes: my confirmation suit.
The "Green Knight" tie I went hungry to buy.
Grandpa's bowler.
Grandma's apron and her fox fur.
Mother's starched white nurse's uniform.
Uncle Irl's riding britches.

That should begin to give you the idea of subjects breaking down into topics and how topics begin to accumulate. Amusements, activities, games, entertainment, toys, clothing. . . . You could add treasured possessions, objects found and lost, equipment, tools . . . and you might arrive at Grandfather's pocketknife.

Travel and Transportation

The obvious topics are cars, trucks, trains, bikes, boats, horses, wagons, donkeys, donkey carts, dogcarts, dogsleds, streetcars, subways, airplanes, balloons, dirigibles, roller skates, and magic carpets. I've read a woman's report on how her family came by train and buckboard to their North Dakota homestead around 1910; a young girl's story about her first sailboat ride; and a Japanese man's memory of his first streetcar ride after coming to America. One woman wrote a short story about a priest traveling by dogsled in Alaska. I might write about how my grandfather worked for the railroad. Or I could write about my first airplane ride in a small Piper Cub. How about hitchhiking and ambulances? Tramways and chair lifts? My mother used to tell about how she was in an automobile accident when she was six months pregnant with me. That's good for a couple of pages.

Let me take the subject of boats from the list and carry the topic breakdown further:

1. We lived near the Big Muddy River and often built rafts to float on the river. One flood season we found an abandoned rowboat. My sister and I paddled it out into the flood-swollen river, using our hands for oars.
2. While I was in the military, I traveled to Europe and back on troop ships.
3. I learned to sail while I was in college.
4. A partner and I operated a boat sales and charter business for a time.
5. I have never been able to teach my wife how to sail.
6. I remember exactly where we were when my daughter Romy caught her first fish.
7. When we had a heavy summer rain, the neighborhood kids and I floated toy boats in the street gutters.
8. I bought my first boat in the dark. It was moored in Poverty Bay, was half-full of water, had a flat bottom, a concrete keel, and green canvas sails. It cost me dearly in time, money, and lost friendships.
9. As kids, we built toy boats—flat pieces of wood with sticks for masts and paper for sails. I built a

stern-wheeler with a flat board and a rubber band to drive a flat paddle wheel. I was also big on model airplanes, the type that were assembled from framers and narrow strips of balsa wood and covered with tissue paper and "dope." Finally I decided to build a full-scale airplane based on what I knew of models. That project filled six months of my life and our back porch.

The point here is simple: Let the ideas and topics flow. Jot down almost anything that comes to mind. Be specific about it. If it seems like a small or an insignificant idea or event, that's a good sign. Topics for family histories and memoirs are rarely too simple. But they are often too vague. If the topic is general, make it particular. If it is abstract, make it concrete. If it is big and broad, make it small. The general, the abstract, and the broad are unwieldy and unrewarding topics. Start with the small, plain, simple, specific objects and events; let people and themes emerge from them.

Food

Food is not only a rich source of vitamins and calories, it is also a rich source of topics. Start again with free association; let one idea trigger another. You don't have to have an orderly list of topics. Start with whatever comes to mind on the subject of food. For example, I might start with my daughter Romy's first birthday cake, which came from a mold in the shape of a smiling hippopotamus. When we sat it down in front of her, she put both hands in the middle and began pulling it apart, cake flying in all directions.

On birthday cakes: I have a photo of myself at the age of three, next to a cake shaped like a reclining lamb. That lamby cake was something my Grandmother Hofmann made for me every birthday until I was seven. When I was older and had my first children, I went looking for a similar cake mold and found one. It has become a tradition for most of the girls and me to have lamby cakes for birthdays (Romy's hippo has a story, too). My daughters and their children will be happy to know where the lamby-cake tradition came from.

Look for some topics like that. Any food traditions in your family? Family traditions connected with holidays or religious events and celebrations?

Did you ever steal any food? St. Augustine did, and he made much of it in his confessions.

During the Depression of the 1930s, we lived with my mother's family in Texas part of the time. We lived off the land, often poaching game out of season. We hunted deer, wild turkey, and quail. We robbed the turkey nests of eggs, and my Grandmother Birchfield hatched them in her hen house. Then we "domesticated" the wild turkeys.

In that same period we harvested wild plums and preserved them. One fall I can remember the butchering and the rendering and the making of sausage late into the night. We used the cleaned intestines for sausage casings, and some of the sausage we fried in patties and placed in tins and poured hot grease over them. Buried in grease, they kept for months, preserved, going only a bit rancid toward the end. We used such systems of preservation because we had no electricity for refrigeration.

What can you say about iceboxes? Canning? Smoking? Drying? Salting?

Food: natural foods. I have a friend who grinds his own wheat flour. The flavor is truly distinctive. I raise vegetables and fruits. I could write about the family gardens I've seen in Missouri, Illinois, Kansas, Texas, Oregon, and Washington. Each family branch and each area had its own garden tricks and techniques. A very early memory that comes to mind is of a distant relative trying desperately to save the chickens during a severe cold spell—they lived with him in the house for a couple of weeks. I mean, they had free run of the house!

My Grandmother Hofmann harvested wild plants. The only two I remember clearly were poke greens and dandelion greens, but almost everyone harvested wild persimmons and walnuts and pecans. I'll spare you my story about persimmons.

Food: markets, stores, merchants, vendors. The Seattle Public Market; street markets in Paris; cockle vendors in Norwich, England.

In this and all the topics, keep the human element strong. For example, when I was in grade school in Illinois, we had an old man who drove an ice-cream wagon around town in the summer. I remember him as gray-haired, mustached, and very gentle. I remember some of the kids who would eat half an ice-cream cone and then sprinkle a little dirt on it and complain to him about the dirt in his ice cream. He would give them a new cone.

I never did that, but I did once break into the old livery stable just before it was torn down, and there was the ice-cream wagon and the horse—the only horse-drawn vehicle still in town. My friend and I crawled into the loft and found sacks of grain. One ruptured sack had spilled its kernels onto the floorboards of the loft, and we pushed them through a knothole and watched them stream into a box in the stall where the horse was kept. I think we must have funneled nearly half a bag of grain through that knothole, and the horse was on the verge of foundering when the old man came to the stable and caught us. He was still gentle, even in his scolding. Somehow that made my guilt all the greater.

Forbidden Topics

And that brings us to a major question about all the topics that come to mind: Are there some things best left unsaid? I confess to you my vandalism in the livery stable.

St. Augustine confesses the theft of pears. I admit to my family's poaching of game. There are worse things in my family history, and there is always the question of, "How far should I go in revealing uncomplimentary things about myself and others?"

For me, one main criterion is this: I should not reveal more about others than I am willing to reveal about myself. As a child and as an adult, I have done things I am sorry for and ashamed of. I would confess those things that have taught me a lesson, so that my readers could learn from my mistakes. If those examples of flawed conduct would help them better understand me, then I would reveal them. If in knowing me better, they come to understand human nature better and ultimately come to understand themselves better, then the revealing has served a purpose.

Once an elderly woman asked me, "Do you think we should write about sad things?"

"Yes," I answered, "if you think they have value or offer understanding. Ask yourself whether your great-great-grandchildren would want to know this about their ancestors."

"What if it was something that was against the law?"

"You have to decide. Is the person still alive?"

"No, both are dead. But their children are still alive and live in the same valley."

"Tough question; particularly since I don't know exactly what you are talking about."

"What if it's about murder?"

Believe me, I didn't have enough wisdom to answer that question, or legal expertise. But I will tell you that six months later that same woman turned in to me the first draft of her story about a cousin who had married a violent and jealous man who considered her his property. After several beatings the young woman ran away to her family's house. Her husband came for her and took her home and said he would kill her if she left him again. Her brother said he would kill the husband if he beat his sister again.

Three months later the young woman came again to her family's house, beaten and frightened, saying that her husband was riding after her. The brother went to meet him. Several days later the husband's body was found near the side of the trail. The case was never prosecuted, the woman and her brother are now dead, and so is her second husband.

That series of events occurred in the early 1900s. I think the woman was wise to write about it. It is remote enough in time to have cooled off; the principal characters are dead and will not suffer by the revelation. Most important, the woman did not say the brother killed the husband; she reported only a sequence of events that might lead to that conclusion. The story is meant for a family audience, not the world. (I've omitted the names and places on purpose.) My bet is that future generations of her family will be thankful that she recorded this story and preserved it.

In this matter of forbidden topics, as in all other compositional decisions, the final judgment is yours. Do what seems comfortable and right.

But as you make out your list, don't be too inhibited. Don't worry if the topic is embarrassing or revealing or questionable. Don't worry if it seems trifling, simple, or silly. List it. You need never write about it until you are ready, but if you ever are ready, it will be there to remind you.

Topic Lists

By now your topic list should be taking shape. When I am sitting with a group in a memoir-writing workshop, I often ask them to share their topic lists, because seeing

what one person lists may suggest something to another.
In that vein here are portions of several lists:

woodbox—kindling
tops—string/jacks
marbles (aggies)
handmade sled
the porch glider
butter churn
butter mold
curling irons heating in
  the lamp chimney
block matches
men's elastic armbands
big signs (ads) painted
  on barn roofs
weathervanes
hand-wound
  phonograph
brakeman walking atop
  RR cars
RR cars joined by link
  and pin
hand-operated switches
  for side tracks
snow sheds on railroads
boot-black stands
cigar-store Indians
revolving barber poles
skate keys
pompom pullaway
run sheep run

hammock
a series of dogs, cats,
  rabbits, pigeons,
  banties
my pony
homemade lye soap
sad iron
goose grease
court plaster
section hand
poor farm
Chautauqua
R R time
Stoughton bottle
wooden sidewalks
washing the cream
  separator
sawdust floors of
  butcher shops
dust ruffle at bottom of
  dresses
pie cupboard
sulphur and molasses
  (spring tonic)
velvet portiers
large family portraits
Victrola (His Master's
  Voice) with
  cylindrical records

Andy over
keep away
release (a prisoner
    game)
tag
toss tag
king of the hill
drama club
Christmas pageant
seeing my first opera
the first movie I
    remember
Sunday-night radio
Memorial Day speeches
    and drills
blacksmith shop
Harvey house
Chivaree
belling
smoking cornsilks
Hoosier cabinet
Inkwells in school
    desks
mumbledypeg
pen wipers
slates
slate rags
slate pencils
handmade swing board
wooden-wheel skates
tree swing (at
    Grandma's)

shell collection
canary
door transoms
sliding window screens
stilts
scooter made from an
    old box and
    roller-skate wheels
wooden tubs
burlap wall covering
rain barrel
tar soap
tin-can lanterns
egg ships
outdoor privy
glass milk bottles with
    flat caps
Tank houses and
    windmills
bone dishes and butter
    tops
carpet beaters (sound?)
kerosene lanterns
    (smell?)
smelling salts
Sen-Sen
traction engine
tables of fruit drying in
    the sun
boys with pockets
    bulging with marbles

Up to this point we have been working with lists of objects and actions. They are often the easiest things to remember and jot down because they fall into familiar categories like toys, pets, clothing, games, and the like. Those objects and activities can remind us of certain people and certain experiences that we might write about. Keep your list growing, but if you need additional stimulus, add some of the following:

ECONOMICS
jobs
wages
rents
debts
employers
employees
prices
profits
cottage industries

EDUCATION
Bible classes
nursery schools
home study
grade school
high school
college
fraternities/sororities
night school
military school
homework
teachers
textbooks

clubs and groups
tests and testing
cheating
school lunches
school vacations

ARTS, CRAFTS AND HANDICRAFTS
sewing
painting
cabinetry
ceramics
landscaping
collections
whatnots
music
cooking

LAW AND LAW ENFORCEMENT
illegal acts
arrest
church law
libel

robbery
arson
inheritance
wills
jury duty
riots
prison
police
security guards
military police
customs agent

FAMILY CUSTOMS AND
TRADITIONS
Sunday morning
Saturdays
New Year's Day
birthdays

anniversaries
picnics
travel
food
courtship
vocation
superstitions

SPORTS
swimming
horseback riding
horseshoes
cornhusking
baseball
basketball
hiking and climbing
camping
boating

None of these lists is meant to be complete or comprehensive. Continue to add any subject area that is appropriate, and then work on the topic breakdown.

Feelings, Thoughts, Ambitions, Emotions, Hopes, Fears

These are often difficult subject areas because they are abstract. In most cases you will be better off writing about a horseback ride that frightened you than writing about fear itself. Poverty is an abstraction; not having enough money to buy medicine for a sick baby or to buy food or pay bus fare is specific. In writing about the specific incident, the abstraction will become clear.

That's no reason for not listing some of your hopes and fears and ambitions, but don't write about them as abstract or philosophical ideas. Write about experiences and observations and dialogues that reveal those thoughts and ideas. For example, a woman in one of my seminars had been raised as an only child and regretted never having any brothers or sisters. Now, had she written about *loneliness,* she might have said,

> "I was always very lonely as a child; I never had anyone to play with. I always wished I had a brother or sister to play games with. But my mother and father had decided that one child was all they wanted. I believe that it's better for children to grow up with other children around them. Being an only child is a terrible thing."

The reader ends up with the general idea that the writer wasn't happy about being an only child. But the reader doesn't feel much, and we don't understand what it was like; we don't know what experiences the writer had.

But the writer wisely let us share her childhood experiences. She wrote about her father's ministry and how his work in the church made her isolation and loneliness worse because he was reassigned every year or two, and the family moved from town to town. The little girl lost her old friends and had to make new ones. She described her mother packing the family possessions and unpacking them in the new parsonage. And in the most poignant scene of all, she described her joy at having a young girl stay with them overnight, and her hope that the parents would adopt her as a companion for their daughter.

The point to be made here is that you can list any idea or thought or feeling as you are working up your topic list, but think beyond the idea or abstraction to the specific experience that will illustrate it. Think of the story that will help your reader *see* and *feel* and *understand* as you did.

Stories, Tales, Narrative, Anecdotes, and Sayings

Almost every family and group has its familiar tales and yarns, the do-you-remember-when stories that get kicked around and told over and over. Use them. Add them to your list.

For example, I've often repeated the story about the time during the Depression that my uncle and his crew harvested the tomato crop. The sheds and yard were stacked with hundreds of boxes of tomatoes, red ripe and near rotting, but there was no market for them. It cost more to ship them than they would bring in. So they sat there, waiting to be fed to the dairy cattle.

I was five and came outside after my Saturday afternoon bath, waiting for the trip into town with my mother and grandmother. The hired hands were fooling around, their labors done. One of them threw a tomato. Another responded. I got into the act. Within seconds the air was filled with flying tomatoes as grown men let off steam, venting their anger and frustration at an unjust world, and a little boy enjoyed it to the hilt.

Mom and Grandma came scolding, and everyone simmered down. I still remember my mother fussing about the tomato seeds in my ear and how my good white shirt and pants were ruined. "Tomato Fight" goes on my list. Even after I write that story, I can go on telling it. But when I'm dead and gone, what I write will keep speaking for me. Down the line somewhere is a future generation I'll never know, but they will know a little about me and about where they came from.

Then there are the stories you've heard others repeat. Or there are the tales about a house or community or person that have been around for a long time. One writer who grew up in California had heard tales about the gold fields since her early youth. She recorded them as an oral history of the community. Another man remembered his brother, a drifter and something of a black sheep, who told the best stories in the family. He put them on paper.

Sometimes there is only the briefest vignette or anecdote. You might not know exactly how you are going to use it—it will only fill a paragraph or two—but jot it down anyhow. For example, there was a distant relative of ours who had a reputation as a big eater. It was during the Depression, when money and food were short. Cousin Clifford was known as the man who could eat a loaf of bread at one meal, using the slices to slop up anything that was left in the serving dishes. When it was announced that he was coming, the typical remark was, "Hide the grub; Clifford's in town." During the year if someone asked, "What should we do with the leftover potatoes?" the answer was likely to be, "Save 'em till Cousin Clifford comes."

Family sayings and expressions are worth recording, particularly if you know how they got started.

The First, Last, Best, Biggest, Worst

Take any topic and think of the first or best or biggest. I've already mentioned "My First Tuxedo" and "My First Boat." You could write about your first job; your worst failure; your best teacher or your best subject in school; your favorite reading; or the happiest, saddest, or scariest moment you can remember. If all else fails just write about an event that is strong and clear in your mind. It wouldn't be strong and clear if it didn't have some distinction. You don't have to give it a name or fit it into a category—just write about it. Make it your very first bit of memoir or family history.

Mnemonic Devices

Up to this point we have been talking about subjects breaking down into topics and how to list them in a random, free, open manner. If something comes to mind, put it down. Free association, free flow of memory will deliver a bounty of writing topics. Whatever comes to mind, list it.

However, there are some other ways to jog memory and expose topics. One of these we've used: It is thinking in categories and classes and types and groups. You remember Grandma's homemade fruitcake and you start to list pastries. Grandma also made doughnuts. Mama favored upside-down cake. Easter chocolates. If that suggests holiday foods, then you list Easter eggs, Fourth of July picnic lunches, Christmas candy, birthday cakes, Halloween candies and treats, and so on. But here are a few more devices to help energize your brain cells.

Questing. Who, what, when, where, why, how? Ask questions about the origin of things, how they were acquired or disposed of. For example, the Easter eggs: Who colored them? How? When? Where? Where were they hidden? Or how were they distributed? Who did it? When was the hunt? Write about your Easter-egg hunt, or your son's or your sister's.

Examine an object. When I was a boy I had a BB gun. Where did it come from? When did I get it? How long did I have it? Where did I keep it? How did I use it? What did it look like? How did it operate? Where did I get BBs and how much did they cost? What did I shoot at? What finally happened to it?

Have you ever seen the movie *Citizen Kane?* It opens with a deathbed scene in which the great man Kane lets fall a paperweight filled with water in which snowflakes swirl. He mutters the word "Rosebud" and dies. The movie unfolds as a reporter tries to find out what or who

Rosebud was. In the final scene of the movie, we discover that Rosebud is the name on the great Kane's sled, a toy from his rural youth in the Rosebud district of Montana. If my dying word is "Daisy," don't go looking for a young lady; it'll be a reference to my Daisy BB gun, the pride of my youth.

Mapping.   Questions about an object should suggest other objects, activities, people, and places about which you might write. But you also can *map* places you have been. For example, map a room you once lived in. Draw a floor plan, and put in doors and windows and furniture. Map a house. Map the yard. Map the outlying fields and buildings, or map the neighborhood in which you lived.

Let me talk you through one of my maps. When we lived with my father's parents, we lived in the house owned by the lumber firm for which my grandfather worked. The lumberyard and offices filled half a city block, except for the lot on which our house sat. To the west was the alley that divided the block. Across the alley was the nice old brick home of the Widow Sharp. (I'll write about her later.) To the north were the lumber sheds and cabinet shop. To the east were the open yards with the sand, gravel, cement blocks, brick, and tile. (I remember a workman we called Black Tom, who made cement blocks on a hand-operated molding machine. Tom and I were good friends, and I'll write a short piece about him.)

Behind the house was a small storage shed. It was L-shaped. On the wall were two shelves that held cans of paint, half-used and forgotten. Once I reached and strained for a bucket of paint, which tipped over. Its lid popped off, and I was covered with green paint. Another time my grandfather had a barrel of lime brought over to the shed from the lumberyard. He had lost a small diamond from his lodge ring when his hand rapped the side of the barrel. My job was to sift through several hundred pounds of lime in that barrel, looking for his small diamond. I never found it, but I breathed in a lot of lime dust.

There are three or four topics arising out of the mapping: the spilled paint, the sifting of the lime, a profile on Black Tom, and another on Mrs. Sharp. And I'm not even into the house yet.

If you draw a map or floor plan, it will trigger your memory of people, places, objects, and events. The map or floor plan might itself become part of your memoir or family history.

Dream-Walking.   Imagine yourself walking from one place to another, from home to school or from home to church or to a friend's house. Or walk from the house to the barn. Or walk to your job. Or walk from one room to another.

As you walk, let the mind's eye fill in as you go. You want to recall every possible detail of the locale. When I went hunting with my uncle in Texas, we walked out through the corral, past the open milking stalls . . . the *open* milking stalls? It's true: Rain or shine, winter or summer, morning or night, he milked twenty cows by hand, out in the open . . . down the dusty wagon road that was all but faded out, past prickly-pear cactus and mesquite trees, past the flooded *caleche* flats covered with a stiff, mosslike plant and populated in the late evenings by hundreds of fiddler crabs who emerged from their dark, damp mud burrows.

I stress the physical act of *walking* in the memory recall because, for me at least, the recall is more vivid if it is associated with action and/or sensation. However, any mode of movement or transportation could work, and so could pretending to sit in one spot and *imaging* everything within the mind's view.

I have found these attempts to visualize locations and past events more productive the more often I do it, and more productive if I push myself to reach for something I don't think I remember. I find it worthwhile to do this for several consecutive nights, for the mind seems to thrive on it; some chemistry is set in motion that persists into the next day. Then images come more easily.

As an example, I closed my eyes one night and said to myself, "Let's walk down that other street . . . Fourteenth Street . . . haven't been there for a while . . . which side of the street? . . . the usual side . . . the first house on the corner was where we lived the year after I was born . . . the second house . . . the third . . . and a couple of more before the alley, under the maple, where we used to set up our lemonade stand in the summer." The next day not only was the lemonade stand a new idea to work with, but so were several other stands and money-making schemes that we got into as kids.

The first few times this approach may not produce a "new" memory or a new topic, but it renews old ground and may help in the development and explanation of some topic.

Using Photographs and Documents. If mapping and dream-walking don't jog your memory, go to the photo album. First there are the images themselves, pictures of people, houses, locales, or events. But look a little closer; search for secondary or hidden details. Study each small part of the photograph. Use a magnifying glass and examine small objects like a watch fob, a bandage on a hand, a battered hat, a scarf, a dog in the background, part of a building or structure—all of which may call up half-forgotten topics or events.

Photographs frame space, so ask yourself, "What is just beyond the edges of the photograph? What part of the world has this image been cut from?" In your mind, go beyond the borders. Ask yourself, "Who took the picture? Where was the photographer standing? What kind of camera was it?"

Photographs are moments in time, so ask yourself, "What happened just before this picture was taken?

What happened afterward? How did the subjects get there? How and when did they leave? Where did they go?"

In addition to photos, there are other documents that might suggest writing topics. Certificates and awards may generate memories of events that could be described or narrated. Report cards, letters, diaries, and news clippings might suggest an incident that could go into a family history. With a little experience you will begin to find writing topics everywhere—I find them in antique shops, rummage sales and museums—and eventually the very act of writing will generate new ideas.

Relatives, Friends, and Fellow Writers. I've saved this group until last because it provides one of the few *social* occasions for the writer, as well as one of the best sources of topic generation. After you've worked on your list for a while, raise a few topics with some other member of the family and see what he or she comes up with that you can add to your list. An old friend or schoolmate may be able to remind you of adventures you had all but forgotten. And, finally, profit from the experiences and ideas of other writers. Join a writing group or form one of your own. I know from the work I have done with groups that one writer's recounting of an early experience will send ripples of recall through the whole group. Sharing your writing with others engaged in the same kind of project is one of the best ways to improve writing, stimulate recall and new ideas, and sustain you through the long private hours.

By now you should have your own ever-expanding list of topics. List every idea or object or person or event that comes to mind. Let the ideas flow. Free associate. Use any device to free up more ideas. Think in categories, groups, and classes. Reconstruct the history of things. Map out houses, yards, fields, and communities. Try the dream-walking exercise, and search out new memories. Re-create in your mind the sights, sounds, tastes, smells, and tactile qualities of an early experience. Become familiar with yourself and your past.

There are a multitude of things, people, places and events, thoughts and feelings that you can write about. But you will not write about everything; you will not have to write it all at once; you do not have to organize it all at once. You will write about small, simple topics that interest you, topics that can be organized and developed in a few pages. If you write for an hour a day, you will begin to capture part of your life. If you want to construct a family history touching upon dozens of lives, do it a piece at a time, page by page.

Your list of topics is begun. Let it continue to grow. But now it is time to write.

Writing

iv Bold, Quick Strokes

The first draft should be written in quick, bold strokes, striving for the essential idea; then form and content can be improved by subsequent revisions.

Life is full of excuses, but nothing generates more excuses than the fear of writing. They go something like this:

1. I don't write very well. I'll leave the writing to someone else. (Most people will say the same.)
2. I don't know what to write about. Or, I don't have anything to say.
3. Most of my ideas are simple and uninteresting. They're not important. (We've said that *significance* is a false and unreliable guide. Simple, honest observation will do.)
4. I don't want to bore my reader. (Your readers are family who are interested in family. They come with built-in interest. Most of your readers have not been born yet. The child of 2077 will marvel at

the smallest details you provide—the simple, obvious things.)

5. I was never very good at grammar. My spelling isn't very good. (This is the second line of excuse. Old manuscripts are full of misspellings. The grammar is quaint and irregular. No one cares; we read them for their information and spirit, not their mechanical excellence.)

6. I don't have time. I can never find the time. (You need no more than 30 to 60 minutes per day.)

I have used all these excuses for years, and sometimes I still try to use them. Most of my friends and students use them. Read about professional writers, and they will admit to a strange array of exotic excuses.

There are no easy answers. You simply must decide to write.

But I can give you some advice and a little inspiration, which may help. The first is the realization that your attitude toward writing is not much different from anyone else's. You would like to write, but your fears and excuses keep you from it. It is hard to start writing, but once you get started, it is a little easier. Done on a regular basis, writing is not so formidable. Thirty to sixty minutes a day is all you need. If you found time to read this book, you can find time to write.

I've had students say, "It's easy enough for you. You like to write." Mostly I like to eat. I also like to sail, to travel, to be entertained, to gossip with friends, to read, to hunt and fish, and to garden and play with the kids. First thing you know, there aren't enough hours in the day for writing. It's easy to put off writing if you think of it as something you may or may not like to do. It's okay to like writing, but the truth is that *you will write when you finally realize that writing is the only way to achieve the goals you desire.* If there were a better way to communicate the things I want to say, I would use it. But there isn't any more efficient or economical way, so I write.

The excuses are always there if you allow them to be. And the last big, phony excuse is *inspiration.* The notion of inspiration must have been created by someone who was running out of excuses and had to face the task. In a moment of desperation he created the inspired excuse: "I can't write unless I'm inspired." If you devote yourself regularly to the making of words on paper, you, too, may become inspired, *but writing precedes inspiration, not the other way around.*

So go and write. Whatever you put on paper will be better than nothing; each sentence is a success.

There are no principles of composition, no rules of grammar to worry about. All the principles of writing— except one—are important when you come to rewriting, but in the first writing—in the first draft or rough draft —the only principle that counts is that you must write.

Choose any of your topics or ideas. It doesn't matter where you start. Pick one you like. Pick a topic that is easy and familiar. Don't worry about being inspired or creative or original or clever. No one is going to read your rough draft. People will read your revised drafts.

Write. Five paragraphs, six paragraphs. Get the rough shape of the idea down on paper. The rest of this book will tell you how to improve on your first draft, but you already know all there is to know about the writing of the first draft. *Every person is capable of writing the rough draft the way it should be written.* Others can tell you how to rewrite, and every writer can learn more about the craft and the art of revision. But you know all you need to know to do the rough draft.

Write. Don't expect miracles or inspiration or perfection. In Greek legend Athena was born beautiful, strong, and fully formed, springing from the head of her father, Zeus. Venus emerged from the sea perfect, fully developed. Things like that happen occasionally among the gods and in the world of myth. In human experience almost nothing takes form that way: Perfection in writing rarely appears before the ninth revision. But the writer can let his or her work spring forth in rough, imperfect form. By letting the material take shape and form quickly, it is born, at least. Then the writer can nurse it to perfection through revision.

Write. There may be a magic to writing, but it is a magic that exists within yourself. There is no magic in this chapter or in the rest of the book that is as great as the magic in yourself.

Write. Don't wait for inspiration; it is waiting for you! Inspiration will meet you when you are half-finished with the revision.

Write. Don't bother reading further until you have written something. The rest of the book is for writers who must rewrite. If you have the time to read further, you have the time to write, and the time is now.

Rewriting

v Prospects for Change

> Writing is an act of continual judgment and selection. You decide what to write about, where to start, the first word, then the second word. . . . In one sense you revise even as the first word goes onto paper. What we call revision is the more obvious process of judgment and selective change that follows the first rough draft.

If the agony is too great, you don't have to revise at all. If you've got some words down on paper, you are already ahead of the game. If you did nothing but write rough drafts, it would be better than writing nothing at all. Your readers could learn something from them.

You don't have to revise immediately. You can write rough drafts on six or seven different topics before you go back to one of them to revise it. Postponing revision will give you a chance to develop a feel for your material, and it will keep you moving forward. It will give you a little distance and some objectivity, both of which are helpful in the revision process. If you don't want to revise right now, keep writing on new topics. Come back to this book for a discussion on revision when you need it.

Revision Is Uncomplicated

The hardest things about revision are the false notions and misconceptions we have about the process. Therefore we can make revision easier and more effective if we eliminate some of the worst notions.

1. The most common error about revision is that it is drudgery. The line of thinking seems to go something like this: If writing can be compared to cooking a meal, then revision is washing greasy pans and dirty dishes after all the fun has been had. But that's not a true analogy. A better analogy goes like this: The first draft is like making out the grocery list and doing the shopping. Revision is like peeling onions, slicing carrots, and seasoning the stew, that is, *converting the raw materials into a more tasty and digestible form.*

2. Another version of the drudgery gambit is that the first writing is creative, but all rewriting is mechanical. Not true. Every rewrite is creative, for the ideas and the form and the language are constantly being changed and improved. Creativity is an ongoing process, and, in fact, more creativity and originality occur in the various revisions than in the first draft.

3. Some people feel that revision is "following the rules." For such people revision means correcting the spelling and punctuation. In practice, that is the last and, in many ways, the least important concern of revision.

4. Finally, there is the "sad truth syndrome." All of us have experienced the frustration and despair of revising something and then saying, "It's worse than it was before! The more I try, the worse it gets!"

That can happen. But it's not a reason to avoid revision. Clumsy and misguided revision can ruin the best material. Hit-and-miss changes aren't the way to revise. Blind fumbling isn't the answer. If you go at it with a plan, a sense of purpose, and direction, you have a better chance of improving on your rough draft.

The Basic Steps in Revision

Step 1. Make sure the topic and purpose are under control. In a sentence or two write down the central point or main idea in your rough draft. Then ask yourself, "Have I stayed on the subject, and did I say what I thought I wanted to say?" Then ask yourself, "Did I want to summarize this in a few hundred words, or did I want to write in detail about a specific person, place, or event?"

If what you want to write is a summary or overview, then a few hundred words can cover a dozen years. On the other hand, if what you want is a detailed story or explanation, then you will need to narrow and focus your topic. The key question is, "What am I trying to say, and what effect should it have on my readers?" Until that sense of focus and purpose is clear, you can't revise effectively.

We've discussed this problem in great detail in chapters III and VI.

Step 2. If the topic and purpose are clear, the next major question is, "Have I said enough so that both present and future generations will be able to understand?" This question concerns *development* or *completeness.* In most revisions of small, focused topics, it will be necessary to expand or develop the statement with sensory details, description, facts, dates, and examples. Good development will let your audience experience and sense the world as you did.

Development is discussed in chapter VII.

Step 3. Check the overall organization of the piece to see if one paragraph follows another in an orderly way. Check the individual paragraphs for coherence and smoothness. If they are needed, add transitional words and phrases to clarify the progression of ideas.

Some manuals and writing guides would place organization before development in the revision process. In my experience it isn't until the paragraphs are fully developed that you can adequately review their order and their internal continuity. Moreover, organization is less of a problem than topic control and development.

Organization and coherence are discussed in chapter VIII.

Step 4. At this point you can improve the style a bit, spruce up the sentences, and better the word choice. After that correct the spelling and punctuation.

Since you don't have to aim for high style or perfection in grammar or mechanics, you'll find only basic guidelines in chapter IX.

To do all that may take more than one revision. Tackle the problems one at a time in easy, simple steps. A good revision should be closer to what you want to say, and it should be easier to read and understand. But don't make the mistake of comparing your revised work to published material; compare your revision to your rough draft. Your revision is successful if it is better than the first draft. Comparison with professional writers is meaningless.

The main objective of revision is to bring you, your message, and your readers into harmony. That is not a mechanical chore—it is a creative, even a loving, effort. It requires time, thought, energy, sensitivity, awareness, and a lot of trial and error, but it's worth it.

vi Point of Departure

Your writing must have a point, however simple. All advice on how to improve the writing and all effort to improve the writing is useless if the topic is too broad or the purpose poorly understood.

In chapter IV you were advised to limit and restrict your topic; the same advice applies here. If you find from the discussion in this chapter that your topic is still too broad or your purpose not clearly understood, then you should reshape the topic and *write a new rough draft around the revised topic.* That may be hard advice to take, but it is better than struggling with an unmanageable topic.

Your topic may already be under control. If so, you should be able to determine that by studying it in the light of the comments and examples in this chapter. If your topic is in control, then the next step in revising your rough draft is to improve the development, which is the subject of the next chapter.

However, if you try to develop your writing before the topic is under control, or if you try to organize it better or improve the language before the topic is truly work-able, then you will be struggling with the impossible and wasting much time and energy. It would be the equivalent of building a house on a poor foundation: Regardless of how hard you worked, the house would tilt and collapse. A clear topic and purpose are the foundation of your writing. Make sure that they are solidly under control before entering the next phase of revision.

To help you evaluate the topic and purpose in your rough draft, we will consider five interrelated ideas:

1. the distinction between writing a summary and writing a detailed explanation
2. the way in which summary writing works with broad topics, while detailed explanation works with limited, narrow topics
3. the way in which limited topics promote unity in the writing
4. the way in which theme and thesis statement can bring the writing into focus
5. the way in which writing creates an illusion of reality for its audience

Summary or Detailed Explanation

The first question about your rough draft is this: Is it meant to be a summary or a detailed explanation? If it's meant to be a summary, then it will cover a broad subject quickly in a few paragraphs. It may summarize a person's whole life in three or four paragraphs. It may summarize several years in a few hundred words.

For example, I had one writing student, a woman in her eighties, who summarized her enlistment in the Army Signal Corps during World War I, her subsequent overseas assignment in France, her work with the Peace Commission after the war, and her return home—all of that—in about eight pages.

Later she expanded and developed that material into a book. Her first version was a very general summary; her completed book was a detailed explanation of her experiences and observations. Both versions served a purpose, but most readers want the detailed explanation so they can share in the experience and understand it better.

What do you *want* to write? A summary? Or a detailed explanation? You need to know what it is you want to accomplish. As you revise, you need to weigh your intent against what you actually achieved in the first draft.

For example, if I want to write a summary or an overview of my grandfather's life, it would read like this:

John Marshall Hofmann, my paternal grandfather, was born in Haubstadt, Indiana, in 1878. He was baptized and attended school through the eighth grade in nearby Mt. Vernon, Indiana. Some time later he attended Draughon's Business College in Springfield, Missouri.

On February 11, 1901, he married Maude White, and they had four children: Louis, born April 5, 1903, in Paducah, Kentucky; Roy, my father, born October 19, 1905, in Aurora, Missouri; and Howard, born July 9, 1907, in Springfield, Missouri; their only daughter, Mary, was born April 14, 1915, in Springfield, Missouri. She died of pneumonia in 1920 at the age of five.

During his late twenties and early thirties, John Hofmann worked for the Frisco Railroad on the run between Springfield, Missouri, and Fort Scott, Kansas. In February, 1910, on his last run as a fireman, prior to becoming an engineer, he was in a train wreck near Fort Scott. His leg was injured and was later amputated in the Frisco Hospital in Springfield.

He moved his wife and three sons to Pocahontas, Arkansas, in 1917, and he lived there until 1929, working in several lumbering and mill operations.

In 1929 John Hofmann and the company he worked for moved to Murphysboro, Illinois, to help in rebuilding the town which had been nearly destroyed by a tornado. Within a few years he became foreman at the Swafford Lumber Company in Murphysboro and worked there for the next twenty years, until his retirement in 1952. By then his wife, Maude, had been dead for thirteen years, and his two surviving sons, Howard and Roy, had married and moved away.

After retirement he lived briefly with his son, Howard, and his daughter-in-law, Grace, on their farm in Missouri. Then John Hofmann returned to Pocahontas, Arkansas, where he married a former acquaintance, Katherine Davis, a nurse who had cared for his daughter, Mary, during her illness forty years earlier.

In November, 1960, at the age of eighty-two, John Hofmann died.

That's a summary of my grandfather's life. It covers eighty-two years in seven paragraphs. Its main emphasis is on places, names, and dates, and as it stands, it is only slightly more developed than a genealogy. As an introduction to a subject, it is satisfactory, and, in fact, certain writing, such as encyclopedia articles, reports, and biographical sketches, might use this sort of summary beginning to establish background before going into a more detailed explanation of a person's career or contributions.

But as family history or personal memoir, the summary isn't satisfactory by itself—it doesn't provide enough detail. You know very little about my grandfather's personality from the summary I've written. You might wonder how the loss of his leg affected him, or whether the death of his only daughter was an even greater loss, but you can't know from what I have told you so far. Summary writing doesn't let you become very intimate or involved with people. Broad subjects and the summary approach they require keep the audience at a distance.

My grandfather's life as I sketched it suggests dozens of topics, some obvious, some hidden. If I want you to *know* my grandfather intimately, I need to narrow and focus my topic until you can see him more clearly, more closely.

For example, if I want you to know my grandfather the way I knew him, then you'll have to see him as I saw him. That will take time, and it will take several different pieces of writing. So where do I start? In some ways it doesn't make any difference where I start, as long as it's a workable topic. I'm going to start with my grandfather's artificial leg, which we always called his wooden leg. In particular, I'll write about him and his wooden leg from my point of view, as a young boy curious about that odd device that he strapped to his body each morning.

Grandpa's Wooden Leg

John Hofmann, my grandfather, worked as a fireman on the Frisco Railroad between Springfield, Missouri, and Fort Scott, Kansas. In 1910, when he was thirty-one, he was in a train wreck which caused the loss of his right leg.

Years later, when I knew him, he never spoke much about the accident, but when I was about seven, during the time we lived with him and my grandmother, I would watch him lashing that wood, metal, and leather contraption to his thigh, and I would ask, "Grandpa, what happened to your leg?"

"I wore it down to a stub, can't you see?"

It was true—there was a tapering stub about eight inches below his knee. It looked and felt like a horse's nose, and in the evenings after work, Grandfather would often take off his wooden leg and massage the stub. I would ask, "Does it hurt, Grandpa?"

"Kinda itches," he would say. "Sometimes the big

toe itches so bad I want to scratch it off, but I can't reach that far. Can you reach your big toe?"

"Sure, that's easy."

"Could you reach it if it was three hundred miles away?"

"How could it be?"

"Mine is. Three hundred miles away and six feet down."

When he talked that way it sounded spooky, and I'd quit asking him questions, which is probably what he wanted. But I never gave up on the topic, and one day I asked my grandmother what happened to his leg and she said, "It was that doctor. He was a company man and knew more about whiskey and womanizing than medicine. He was liquored up when they brought your grandpa in after the accident."

She talked without stopping her work in the kitchen, speaking into the mixing bowl rather than looking at me. "Your grandpa was injured in the wreck, got his leg caught in the coupling, smashed the calf muscle, and when the doctor saw it, he said it was too badly damaged to repair, too much likelihood of blood poisoning, he said, even if the bone was all right. So he just sawed your poor grandfather's leg right off. It was all done 'fore I knowed of it."

About that time she got a little touchy on the subject, and I could tell she was sad and angry and maybe going to cry. The beating in the mixing bowl got more furious, and she looked up at me and said, "Seems everything's done and settled before I know about it." But then she dropped the subject like it wasn't fit for my ears. "Make yourself useful," she said. "Run down to the store and get me a bottle of vanilla extract . . . and yourself a penny candy . . . and move your wagon off the front walk 'fore a body breaks their neck."

My curiosity might fade then for a while, but that leg wasn't forgotten. It was there in the slight limp and clump of my grandfather's walk, something so slight that many people thought he had just a sore foot or a bad joint. Sometimes there was a faint squeak at the heavy metal hinge at the knee joint or at the ankle joint. My grandfather would get out the oil can, and the leg would quiet down a bit.

But there was always the dry squeak and crunch of leather about that leg. First, there was what he called the harness, something like a suspender that went across his shoulder, attached to a heavy leather sheath that clamped around his thigh, and was the main means of attachment. Then his knee joint fit between the squeaky artificial knee hinges, and his stub slipped into the hollow shaft of the artificial lower leg, which was made of laminated or molded wood. At the end of the lower leg was another joint and the fake foot and its shoe. It was that shoe that squeaked the most.

My grandfather would say his right shoe was "dry," meaning it never had any natural warmth or moisture from a living foot. He felt that was one reason it squeaked more than the other shoe. Then, too, it would slip a bit on the artificial foot if he didn't lace it up very tightly.

When I first knew him, he changed shoes on the artificial leg on Sundays, but later he bought a second "Sunday" leg and kept his Sunday shoe on his Sunday leg. That pleased him a great deal, and I thought his Sunday walks had a bit more spring to them.

On at least two occasions that I can remember, Grandpa's artificial leg saved him from injury. One day while he was working in the lumberyard, my grandfather was supervising the unloading of a truck. One of the beams toppled off and crashed down on his foot, the artificial one. He couldn't move until the workmen lifted the beam off, but he had no injury, and the leg wasn't damaged.

Later that evening at supper he retold the story of how the truck driver, a stranger, had helped remove the beam and kept exclaiming, "Call a doctor! Take off your shoe before that foot swells! Mister, you better take off that shoe and check for broken bones. It'll swell for sure." The other yard men who knew about Grandpa's leg got to laughing fit to be tied. The driver thought they were all crazy and told them so.

Another time Grandpa came in at the rear door on the back porch, clumping up the steps to stomp off the cement dust that was all over his shoes and pants. The dog had been sleeping on the back porch, and when the stomping started and he saw this dusty figure looming over him, he growled and snapped at the leg. I guess he connected with his teeth, because he stopped in his tracks and looked puzzled. Grandpa swung the leg, and he connected with the dog's shoulder and sent him flying down the steps and ki-yiing away. Grandpa could be a bit ornery if the mood was on him.

I think by the time I knew him, my grandfather had come to accept that wooden leg as a natural part of his life. By then he had had it for better than twenty years, and his friends knew about it, and strangers were completely unaware of it. Old friends would ask, "How's the leg today, John?" and Grandpa might say, "Standing up," or "It's got a few miles left in it." I could never figure whether they were talking about the real one or the wooden one, but that didn't seem to matter.

On at least one occasion I remember somebody

asking Grandpa how he felt, and he replied, "Pretty fair for somebody with one foot in the grave," and he looked sly and winked at his friend and moved on. I remember the man's wife looking concerned and saying in a whisper, "Is Mr. Hofmann ill?" Grandpa would have loved that.

The Limited Topic Permits Detailed Explanation

The first example was a summary, a sweeping survey of my grandfather's entire life. The second example is a developed explanation of one factor in my grandfather's life: his wooden leg. The entire life is a broad topic. The leg is a narrow, limited topic. The broad topic forces me to summarize and to skip over many things. The narrow topic forces me to look closely and remember small details and intimate events.

While both summation and explanation have their purpose, and while both may be interesting, it is the detail and immediacy of the explanatory writing about the leg that will have the greatest lasting effect on the family audience. That is the reason you are advised to limit your topics and focus closely on small, intimate, and personal details. There is nothing wrong with writing a summary as a background statement or as an introduction, as long as you balance it with several smaller topics that are thoroughly developed.

Let me illustrate this principle further by outlining a few more memories I have of my grandfather:

1. Eating habits: he had some strange food preferences. He liked raw oysters and raw eggs; he would put Limburger cheese on Grandma's hot apple pie; he loved buttermilk. He kept a bottle of rock 'n' rye whiskey in the top of his closet so it was handy for a daily nip.

2. Transportation: he sold his car during the Depression and thereafter never drove again, always walking to church or the lodge hall or an occasional movie. If he traveled any distance he went by train. He hated the bus.

3. Amusements: he played cards every week. When my grandmother was alive, they played pinochle with their friends on Wednesday nights. On Friday nights they would often turn out for bingo at the lodge hall. And on Sundays Grandpa and his cronies at the Knights of Columbus would sit down to five or six hours of serious poker playing.

   He enjoyed radio programs, particularly baseball, prizefights, and dramas like *Mr. District Attorney, Gangbusters,* or *Fibber McGee and Molly.* On Sunday nights he was always home in time to listen to Walter Winchell.

Each of these could be expanded to become a little "snapshot" of my grandfather. Admittedly, most of this material is of little interest to a mass audience, but it is the type of thing that is meaningful in developing the image and character of a person within the context of a family history. In fact, it is probably the only way we can get to know a *person* instead of some vital statistics.

Look again at your rough draft and decide if you want a summary overview or a detailed explanation. A detailed explanation is possible only if you have a limited, focused topic. If the topic isn't limited, you won't be able to manage all the details, just as I wouldn't be able to tell everything about my grandfather in one lump of writing.

And you need not worry about a shortage of details. The next chapter is going to tell you how to develop and expand your topics. But even at this stage of controlling the topic, details will start emerging from the woodwork of your mind. An interesting change takes place in writers when they stop thinking in broad, general terms and start thinking of limited, tightly focused topics. They *see* things they didn't remember before. For example, I never remembered that "harness" or suspender my grandfather attached to his leg until I was into the actual process of writing that paragraph of description. I simply didn't know that detail was in my mind until it popped out when I needed it.

Try this: Think of yourself standing in the street or roadway, looking at the house you lived in when you were twelve. Just standing outside, looking at the house.

Your image of the house is like a broad or generalized topic. If you were going to write about it, you should break it down into parts or sections that are more manageable. Let's skip the outside of the house, which might be one whole area of discussion and description, and limit ourselves by moving inside. Let's move right along to the kitchen. Stop at the doorway. Remember the kitchen? In my grandfather's house we ate in the kitchen. Funny, it was known as Grandfather's house, but it was known as Grandma's kitchen.

Let's limit our vision further. Where is the icebox? What do you remember about that icebox? Some of you had a wooden one; when I was twelve, ours was white enameled metal, but still an icebox, not a refrigerator. In the winter we also had a "window box," a small chest that hung outside in the cold but was accessible through a window in the kitchen.

Notice how there is always detail to fill in the picture? You move from house to kitchen to icebox; the focus narrows, but there are always things to talk about, small topics that might require only a few hundred words to explain fully.

Open the icebox. In the summer ours had a water bottle, so we could serve chilled water at mealtime. And there was usually a bowl of Grandma's homemade cottage cheese. Maybe I'll want to write a page or two about how she made the cottage cheese and saved the whey to use in her homemade bread.

Observe the process we have followed. It is similar to the one outlined in chapter III. The message is the same: Whether you are preparing to write or preparing to rewrite, you want a topic that is under control, in most cases a small, narrowly focused topic that you can explain fully in three to fifteen pages.

The Limited Topic and Unity

One of the big advantages of a narrow topic is that it is unified—everything fits together tightly; everything mentioned relates to one idea. It's hard to get off the subject if the topic is small. Unity is important in writing. It is not always present in speech or normal conversation. People sitting around talking may skip quickly from one topic to the next every thirty seconds. But good writing doesn't skip around or wander off the topic. It unfolds and develops a single, central idea.

Unity is a very old compositional guideline that goes back to the ancient Greeks. In their dramas they employed a principle known as the unities of time, place, and action. We can employ the same principle in the writing of memoirs or family history: Focus your topic so that it covers no more than a day in time; or focus the topic so that it is tied to one place—a kitchen, for example; or focus on a single line of action, such as Grandmother making cottage cheese.

A quick example of such unity on a focused topic would go like this:

> Grandfather's amusements
> > playing bingo
> > listening to radio

        playing cards
           pinochle
           poker

Take "poker." I'll write about his Sunday-afternoon (unity of time) poker sessions (unity of action) with his cronies in the Knights of Columbus lodge hall (unity of place). Notice that "playing cards" implies a unity of action, but it is a general category of activity, whereas "poker" is a more specific activity. Specific topics are usually best.

The K. of C. Poker Club

Almost every Sunday, after the family had finished the noon meal of chicken and dumplings and paid their compliments to Grandma's cooking, Grandpa would head for the bedroom. There he would change to his second-best suit, have a nip of his rock 'n' rye whiskey, don his bowler, and leave for the lodge-hall poker session, but not without a quick peck on the cheek for Grandma and not without her warning him to quit if he lost more than five dollars.

He lived only three blocks from the lodge hall, and Grandpa walked there within minutes. The lodge hall was on the second floor, above a paint and wallpaper shop and a Greek restaurant. The stairwell between the two stores, dark and smelling of beer, tobacco smoke, and greasy food, was like a sordid and sinister passageway. But the upstairs was rather light and airy, with tall windows around the north and west walls of the barroom, where the gaming tables were located.

It was a large room with a dozen round wooden tables scattered about, six or seven bentwood chairs per table, and another thirty or forty chairs lined along the east wall. There were ceiling lamps above each table and spittoons on the floor around the tables. The bar, simple, dark wood, angled short and squat across the northwest corner of the room.

In the early afternoon, when my Grandfather and his friends played, only their table and perhaps one other would have a game going. They usually sat along the west wall, above the street that overlooked the Illinois Central Railroad tracks. In summer, when the windows were open, the train smoke would come billowing in through the windows unless the bartender was alert and timely enough to slam them shut before the four-forty arrived. But to an old railroad man like my grandfather, that was hardly reason for concern, and it never interrupted his game.

He and his friends played a serious and rather sober game of poker, careful of the rules, never betting out of turn, never talking extraneously when the betting was on. Indeed, they would begin a conversation when the cards were being shuffled and dealt, then pause while the hand was played out, and then continue the same dialogue through the next shuffle and deal. They joked and gossiped, but not when there was money on the table.

If there was a baseball game on the radio that afternoon, it was the bartender's job to listen, quietly, and report scores during the shuffle. Only when it was a tight ninth inning would the radio go loud and the poker game pause while the St. Louis Cardinals or the St. Louis Browns or the Chicago Cubs drove their man home. Then the poker players might stretch and take a drink at the bar before settling back to their own ninth inning of play.

Along about five, certainly no later than six, the game would break up. Someone would collect a tip for the bartender; a big winner might buy a round of drinks; a final cigar would light up, a final pinch of snuff, maybe a shady joke or two, and then each man would head for home.

The walk was never hurried. That was the time for reviewing the victories and defeats of the afternoon. If Grandpa won he would admit to part of it. If he had lost he would admit to a small part of that. There had been a time, years earlier in Pocahontas, Arkansas, when Grandpa had lost several thousand dollars and part interest in a sawmill in a high-stakes poker game. That had almost been the undoing of his marriage, and Grandmother, holding all the aces for once in her life, had been able to call the turn: She threatened to take the children and leave him unless he swore to reform on the spot.

On that occasion she extracted one of the few iron-clad promises Grandfather ever made; he would never again play high-stakes poker. He kept his promise. Even after she died, he stuck to nickle-dime poker.

This piece has unity. If focuses on my grandfather's Sunday-afternoon poker session. The time period is a matter of four or five hours. The locale, except for the introduction and conclusion, is the lodge-hall game room. While the concluding paragraphs make reference to another time and place, they hold to the unity of action: poker playing.

Look at what you have written and see if any of those unities is in force. "The K. of C. Poker Club" has all three unities operating, but for many topics, one unifying device is sufficient. Think back to the piece I wrote about my grandfather's leg. Does that have unity of time, place, and action? Not exactly. It is not quite correct to say that the leg represents unity of action—it is an object, not an activity. But notice how, even in this discussion, the word *leg* keeps coming up; the unity in that piece on my grand-father's leg is created by the leg itself. We might call it unity of object. Incidents from different times and places can be unified if they all relate to a single, central object. Another example of this principle of unity of object can be seen in Carl Cleveland's piece, "Grandad's Jackknife," in chapter III.

Limited Topics and Thematic Unity

In a similar fashion we can have unity of theme. If I start out saying I want to write about my grandfather, I don't have much selectivity or direction. If you ask me, "What do you want to say about him?" I might answer vaguely, "I want to tell you the kind of man he was." And you might rightly ask, "Well, what kind of man was he?" And I would probably say something like, "He was hard-working, honest, stubborn, set in his ways, fair, something of a gambler, but a bargain hunter, too; fairly religious, had a sense of humor, but he had a temper and could be mean. On the other hand, I've seen him very patient and tolerant." Too much! And it goes in ten different directions at once! The material needs to be limited and focused. It needs to be unified. This time we can use *theme* to narrow and unify the material.

First, I select one of the traits I just mentioned, for example, sense of humor. Second, I write a statement about my grandfather's sense of humor, something like, "My grandfather, John Hofmann, never did funny things or acted foolish, but he had a quiet, sly, ironic sense of humor that emerged in the things he said or in the stories he told." This is the statement of my main point. It is a theme expressed in a *thesis statement.* If I begin my piece with such a thematic statement, it will help focus and unify my writing.

To develop and explain the theme of my grandfather's

"sly, ironic sense of humor," I will set a scene, quote something he said, retell one of his stories, or describe the way he moved or looked. I may, indeed, skip from one day to the next or one year to the next. I may write about him at home, at work, at church, or at the lodge hall. I do not need overall unity of time, place, or action because I have unity of theme, and that is enough to hold the material together and focus it. I have a narrow, limited intent.

The thesis or thematic statement is an excellent tool for beginning certain types of writing, but not all writing. I did not use a thesis statement in "Grandpa's Wooden Leg"; I merely indicated in the introduction that my grandfather had lost his leg and, as a young boy, I was curious about it. I didn't tell you in a thesis statement the main point or idea I was going to communicate, merely that the leg was the topic of discussion.

Nor did I use a thesis statement about the poker sessions on Sunday afternoons. I simply started the narrative with him leaving the house after the noon meal, headed for the lodge hall.

But a thesis statement can be very important if we are interested in writing about an idea, a feeling, or an opinion instead of a narrative or story. When I write, "My grandfather . . . had a quiet, sly, ironic sense of humor," that is my opinion about my grandfather. It is the interpretation I want to convey, and as a thesis statement, it will keep me focused on that theme, keep me from writing about some of his other traits.

Unity and tightly focused topics go hand in hand. A limited topic will have unity of theme; unity of object; unity of time, place, or action. It will have a clearly defined purpose and it will stick to that purpose, providing examples and details that clarify and explain that purpose. It is easier to control unity and focus when the topic is limited and the written statement can be completed in no more than a few thousand words.

Limited Topics and Unity of Perspective

By now you must be getting a little tired of my grandfather and his wooden leg and poker playing, but let me make one more point, this one about unity of perspective. A lot has been written about perspective or point of view in writing, and there is much talk about first-person, second-person, or third-person narration. We don't have to worry too much about that, but we do need to control perspective or point of view in the writing to reinforce overall unity.

For example, in the wooden-leg piece there are lots of *I*'s in the writing. I wrote that piece from my point of view as a young boy observing things and people and participating in the dialogues. I was there in real life, and I was there in the written report.

But in the poker piece there are no *I*'s. It was hard to keep the *I*'s out, let me tell you! After all, I was there in real life, saw what was happening, and on more than one occasion went with my grandfather to the lodge hall (in wide-eyed wonder, not as a gambler).

The point, however, is this: Having decided to stay out of the poker piece, I couldn't write it in the first person, so the entire piece is in the third person. Grandpa and his friends are the subjects of sentences. It would be inappropriate—it would violate the consistency of the piece—if suddenly in the fifth paragraph I were to write, "When I went with him to the lodge hall, he would buy me a cream soda and I would sit at his side, quietly, and watch the cards fall and hear the chips clink into the pot."

The statement is true, and it could make the piece interesting in a different way if I put myself into the account, but if the piece is going to have a first-person narrator, he should be there from the beginning and provide a consistent point of view. Popping into view in the middle of the passage is disruptive and violates the unity of perspective.

Some writers have the mistaken notion that *I* should be left out of all writing. I know of teachers who have told their students that *I* is egotistical or self-centered and shouldn't be used in writing. Well, you can forget that. If the *I* seems natural and appropriate, use it. Especially if you are writing your memoirs or autobiography, you are at the center of action, you are the central subject, and the *I* is a necessity.

Decide on your topic and your purpose, and then decide whether the story or incident is better told from a first-person or a third-person point of view. Experiment with both approaches. Write one piece in the first person and another in the third person and see which feels best and most natural to you. If you are part of the story as you want to tell it, then *I* will tend to emerge on its own. Most writers find it difficult to write about themselves in the third person, and for you and your audience there is little reason to do so. Speak up in your own voice.

But whatever voice you speak in, use it consistently. You don't have to use the same voice in every piece, but in any one piece try to control the perspective or point of view.

Limited Topics and Synthesis of Reality

Another characteristic of the type of writing we are discussing here is that we can "create" unity where none existed in real life. Let's use the wooden-leg piece: In truth, I *compressed,* or *synthesized,* many experiences into one in order to write what I did. After all, I must have seen that leg a hundred times; I heard about it, I asked about it, and on rainy afternoons I would sneak into the closet and play with the Sunday leg. When I wrote the piece, I put together a lot of knowledge acquired over many different days and *made it unified* when in reality my experiences were fragmentary, random, and repetitious.

Take the passage where I quoted my grandfather as saying, "Sometimes the big toe itches so bad I want to scratch it off . . . ." He said that on one occasion. The passage which says, "I wore it down to a stub. . . ." happened another time. I put them near each other *as though they both happened at the same time.* In so doing I created a unified dialogue in which my grandfather says several things about his leg. It makes sense. It could have happened that way. It's more efficient than reality. It makes better reading that way.

Or let me put it another way. My grandfather lost his real leg. He had to make do with an artificial one. The real experience I had with my grandfather has been lost. There is only the question of the artificial one I am able to re-create out of the fragments in my mind. I offer my reader this imitation of the real, historical past.

This raises a point of ethics or morality for some people who will say, "Well, isn't that lying?" My response is, "NO, emphatically not!" It is true that I am trying to combine and unify and condense my knowledge and experience so that it can be easily understood. In so doing, any writer edits and digests his experiences and observations. *The writer seeks not always literal truth or the complete truth, but rather seeks a true impression for his audience.*

You should not expect your writing to be an *exact* duplicate of reality. A photograph is not an exact duplicate of reality; it is an approximate image. The photograph is flat; the real world is three-dimensional. The photograph is a few inches high; the subject it renders is usually several feet tall. The photo may be in black and white, the real world colorful. The photo is unchanging; the real world is dynamic. Subjects are told to smile, even if they have nothing to smile about. People *pose* themselves for photographs. Writers *compose* their material to create a certain impression.

Writing is never a duplicate of the real world. In some

ways it is more valuable than the real world. In the Bible, we read the parable of the Good Samaritan. We know that the parable has been told to us in that form not because the incident is historically true—although something like it may have happened—but because the parable of the Good Samaritan helps us understand the truth and wisdom of helping our neighbor. It is the truth of charity and neighborly love that the parable communicates, not the truth of what was actually said or exactly done.

Give some thought to the truth or impression you are trying to communicate when you write. Your original observations and memories are fused, merged, overlapping, and incomplete in some details. When you write, you must *compose* those thoughts and memories and give them a form and order and directness—yes, and even a clarity—that they did not have in real life. One of the great things you do for your readers is to give them selected information, presented in an orderly fashion to produce understanding and insight. What it may have taken you weeks or months or years to live through and understand, your readers can now live through and understand in a matter of minutes. That is one of the great gifts and economies of writing.

Be at peace with your material and with yourself. We have already removed several burdens from your shoulders as a writer: You are not writing for a mass audience; you are not writing for money; you do not have to satisfy editors and publishers. And you do not have to reproduce literal reality.

As you move through the process of revising your writing, remember our objectives of *plain, simple,* and *small.* Do not try to achieve too much, and do not demand too much of yourself. You have enough work to do as it is. Think now only of your topic. Is it small and clearly focused? Do you have a clear purpose and intent? Do you want to write a summary or a developed explanation? A broad topic will force you to write either a summary or a book. A small, limited, narrowly focused topic can be explained fully in a few thousand words. The small topic will be easier to write.

The rough draft of your material may seem disorderly because it tries to say too much. Look at the possibility of dividing your rough draft into two or three shorter pieces. We have seen how my grandfather's whole life is too complex to be covered except in the most generalized summation. Such a summary or overview may be a good start as an introduction or a beginning, but sooner or later your memoirs or family history must focus on limited, specific concepts or events. You must limit yourself to a series of small topics, each developed individually.

But don't underrate the impact of small topics; they can accomplish much. Even in the short selection on my grandfather's wooden leg, you have learned not only about the leg, which itself is just a curiosity item, but you have learned something about my grandfather. Moreover, you have learned something about me and my grand-mother. And, finally, you have begun to sense something of the atmosphere of the household and the interrelation-ship between members of the family. All of that emerges out of a small, narrow topic expressed in less than 1500 words.

I cannot guarantee that the stories I have written will be meaningful or interesting for a mass audience. But such material is relevant and interesting to present and future generations of my family, and those are the ones for whom it would be written. You are writing for a similar audience.

vii Blind, Deaf, and Numb

Development means saying enough so your reader
can understand and appreciate your message.

If the topic is now limited and better controlled, the next
major step in rewriting is further development. In the first
draft of your writing, you began to explain what you
meant. You began to elaborate, to fill in the details, to
provide the information you felt your audience would
need. That is the beginning of development. In this chapter we want to pursue that development further by over-
coming certain misconceptions and fears, encouraging the
use of more details and examples, and identifying the
sources and forms of well-developed writing.

Development means expanding, examining, and explaining the topic under discussion. Development may
sound contrary to the advice on limiting topics, but, in
fact, it is a complement to that concept. When the topic
is limited, then it is physically and mentally possible to go
into greater and greater detail, to explain carefully and
fully. The first step in the rewriting process is to narrow

81

the topic, and then the second step is to open it up, to go into detail.

Development may seem to contradict the oft-repeated advice to be brief, to get to the point. Brevity is important. Conciseness is important. Directness is important. But completeness and clarity of statement are also important. Therefore, we want to reconcile the apparent conflict between brevity and development. The principle should be expressed this way: *Provide the maximum amount of relevant information in the fewest words in a language the reader can easily understand.*

Don't omit facts, details, and explanations to save words. That misses the point of brevity and damages the development. Keep the maximum information, but write so that three words say as much as four. When writers think brevity means avoiding the details, they are forced to express their ideas in generalizations. When generalizations, opinions, and abstractions are not backed up with facts or examples, they are difficult to understand or accept. Clear explanatory writing consists of approximately ten percent opinion, generalization, and evaluation versus ninety percent facts, examples, sensory details, and definitions.

In typical informational writing generalizations and opinions are found in the introduction, in the conclusion, and in the opening and closing sentences of each body paragraph. The body of the paragraphs and the body of the essay or article should contain the developmental information. So when we talk about developing a piece of writing, we are talking about (1) adding more paragraphs to the body or middle, and (2) adding more details to each of those body paragraphs.

Let's look at a couple of typical examples. Let's say in the rough draft I have written a sentence like, "My grandfather had a wonderful old car we used to ride around in." By itself that sentence says very little; it is vague and undeveloped. It uses the word *wonderful* to express my opinion or evaluation. The word *car* is general and imprecise rather than specific. The clause "... we used to ride around in" is vague. Developing this vague and imprecise sentence might produce a paragraph like this:

> On Sunday mornings Grandfather Hofmann would back his tan 1924 Packard coupe out of the garage and into the alley. While waiting for my grandmother and my sister and me to load up, he would wipe off the light powder of dust accumulated during the week's storage. Grandpa never used the car frivolously; he drove to church on Sundays and home again. Holidays might warrant a visit to a friend or relative. In summer Sunday afternoon might include a picnic or an outing, but that was rare, because Sunday afternoons were reserved for Grandpa's poker sessions. When Grandpa sold the car in the late 1930s, it was still in showroom condition and had less than twelve thousand miles on it.

Notice that the vague sentence has become a developed paragraph that opens up the limited topic: Grandfather's car. In the previous chapter we distinguished between summary statements on broad topics and detailed statements on narrow topics. Here we have a narrow topic in its undeveloped form (the vague sentence) compared to the same narrow topic in a more developed form: one sentence becomes six sentences. If I told you more about the car, how Grandpa drove, and why Grandma didn't, the development would be even better.

When you get the feel for development, you will stop asking, "What can I say?" and start asking, "Where do I stop?" The question is one of selectivity, of judgment. What do I want to say? What does my audience *need* if they are to understand clearly the experiences I want to convey to them? *Writers must select, out of an infinite variety of facts, details, sensations, and examples, the important information that will make the message clear and meaningful to their readers.*

Here, as with most compositional problems, judgment is more important than rules or slogans. *Judgment* is the key word: each writer must develop his or her material according to his or her own judgment—judgment about: "How much does my audience know?" "How much do I know or could I say to make this point clear?" You are successful in your judgment if your reader says, "I understand."

I cannot tell you what to write or how to develop it. I can try to give you a few basic principles, devices, and examples that may help you improve your judgment and the application of your skills. In the end you decide. In a metaphorical sense you decide what lives and what dies. You decide what survives and what is lost. For me, I can tell you that I miss what has been lost of my family history because no one recorded the details.

Sources and Devices

The primary source of developmental details is your memory. Its storehouse of sensory impressions, narrative sequences, feelings, attitudes, and images is infinitely rich. Don't underestimate your memory. Properly encouraged, it can play back for you a symphony of things seen, heard, felt, smelled, or tasted.

We have already discussed a few of the ways you can begin to trigger recall in the process of selecting topics. The same techniques can be used to stimulate the recall of those details that may be important to the development of your writing. Use photographs; use the mapping and dream-walking techniques to help you in the recall of details.

You can also use a kind of deductive logic. In a recent workshop I was talking with a woman who was writing about her experiences as a young teacher in a one-room schoolhouse in the Ozarks. In trying to help her recall details and events related to that experience, I asked her, "What kind of heat did the building have?" She provided details about an old, cranky stove that sat in the middle of the room. I might then have asked, "What kind of fuel did it burn? Who was responsible for lighting the fire on cold mornings? Were there any problems with lighting? Did anyone ever get burned on it? What happened to the ashes? Who disposed of them? Who supplied the fuel? Where was the fuel stored?"

I don't know anything about her specific stove, but I do know that all of those questions apply. I can use my analogous experience with other stoves and a little deductive reasoning (coal or wood would produce ashes) to generate questions which in turn will generate details and, often, new topics. For example, after we had finished with the stove, I asked about the plumbing (there was none) and I then deduced she must have had a water bucket and dipper somewhere for the students. "You must have had your share of problems and pranks with that water bucket," I said. "Oh, let me tell you . . ." she began, and it was obvious that a whole flood of details and incidents were rushing forward for expression. That's what you want—that flood of recall. Questions like who, what, where, when, why, and how will begin the process of generating recall. But sometimes deductive logic is the best device. You may not remember the stairs at your grade school, but chances are there were some. There had to be drinking water. There had to be toilets. And coat racks. You had to eat lunch . . . What kind of lunch? And so on.

I can almost guarantee that you will be awed and delighted by your capacity for recall after you have been practicing it for a little while. What you will have to overcome is not your ability to remember details but your tendency to shy away from the details of development because you are afraid that the details will bore your readers. As long as the details are relevant to the message, relevant to your audience's understanding, they will not be boring.

The second source of information is relatives and friends, but don't depend on them to volunteer specifics. You must encourage them and prod them to remember and develop their statements in the same way that you must encourage and prod yourself. Be an aggressive interviewer, a dogged detective when you ask others for supporting information. You may not use everything they tell you; in practice you may discard part of it. But you don't have any choice about the things that are never said; you may choose only from among the facts that are revealed.

In this case don't depend on your memory to recall the words and ideas of others. When you are seeking information from friends and relatives, take notes and use a tape recorder if it is at all possible. My own experience tells me that during a conversation I can jot down a few key ideas, and I can remember some secondary details, but a lot will be lost if I don't have a tape recorder. Memory loss will be especially severe if much time has elapsed between conversation and writing. For that reason alone the tape recorder is valuable. Moreover, extensive note taking distracts both the writer and the speaker, whereas a small, battery-powered cassette tape recorder with built-in microphone can be quite unobtrusive. (Consult your library for books and pamphlets on oral history and interview techniques.)

Other sources of information are letters, records, documents, diaries, journals, newspapers, magazines, and books. Unfortunately, such sources are rarely as intimate in their detail as we might like. Most of the letter writers in my family talked about the weather, not about their feelings. A marriage license or certificate might provide a few names and dates, but it won't speak of love, devotion, and dreams (or frustrations). Glean what facts you can from those sources, but don't expect documentary research to produce writing as revealing and as human as your own memory can.

One use of such documents is to photocopy them and incorporate them, along with photographs, in your family publication. There they become what can be called graphic development, visual aids to your written statement. A fuller discussion of this subject appears in chapter XI.

From those sources—memory, conversation and interview, and research—you extract sensory details, facts, statistics, examples, descriptions, and explanations that you judge to be relevant and necessary to your readers' understanding of the message. Such information can be called the material or content of good development. But there are also certain devices or approaches to good development:

1. Analysis. By now it should be obvious that I am always breaking topics down into smaller and smaller parts so they can be discussed and explained. That process is *analysis,* the dividing and subdividing into parts. For example, if you decide to write about the family home, you should think of its neighborhood, its land, the house itself, the outbuildings, the basement, the first floor, the second floor, the attic. Then the parlor or living room, the study or workroom, the bedrooms, the furniture, the closets, the hallways and stairs, under the stairs, the kitchen, the nursery . . . or perhaps it is only a two- or three-room flat or apartment, where things are measured in corners and boxes and cupboards; where the bed folds into the wall; or where there is only a cot and a dirt floor. But dirt floor or rich carpet—whatever the environment—you must analyze it piece by part. Only when you see the smaller and smaller parts can you begin to describe

and explain in detail. Small topics and analytical breakdown are the best preparation for good development.

2. Dramatizing or narrating. Fiction writers are advised, "Don't tell the reader, show him!" That's also good advice for memoirs and family history. Where people are involved, let them speak for themselves; let us hear them. Write dialogue. Show them in action.

3. Comparison and contrast. Two of the most familiar devices for developing an idea are *comparison* and *contrast.* If we are trying to explain a person, a place, or an object, it sometimes helps to compare it to a similar person, place, or object. Comparison takes the unfamiliar or new and shows how it is similar to a familiar, like quantity. For example, if I wanted to describe the Kohler plant on my aunt's Wyoming ranch, I might compare it to the motor and generator in an automobile: both are gasoline-powered engines and both drive a generator that produces electricity, but the Kohler plant has a very large generator, which, instead of providing limited 12-volt electricity for a car, provided 110-volt electricity for the barn, tack house, and living quarters.

   You will notice that the foregoing example shifts from *comparison* (both gasoline-powered engines) to *contrast* (large generator for several buildings *vs.* small generator for car's electrical system). Comparison emphasizes similarities, whereas contrast points up differences.

4. Analogy, simile, and metaphor. Analogy is similar to comparison, but an analogy is often drawn between two things that are not like quantities, that is, two things that are basically quite different but that seem to have a few traits in common. In trying to tell about hunting with my uncle, I could draw an analogy between myself and a hunting dog:

I was not quite seven, but Uncle Irl said I could go hunting with him if I could keep up and keep quiet. Mimicking a faithful hunting dog, I trailed close behind him, sometimes trotting to keep up with his long strides, panting in my exertion, pleased and honored to be his companion. If I had had a tail, I would have wagged it, and I have the distinct impression that he would have reached out and patted me on the head.

That is better than saying, "I liked to go hunting with my uncle."

In your writing nothing is more important than good development. It is the very heart and soul of what you have to say. Literally, your words are empty until development fills them. If I sound fanatical on the subject, I am! For if I can release the stored awareness and consciousness and feeling in you, then it will fill your writing and it will flow in richness to your readers, and they will share with you for generations to come.

For other types of writing and for other audiences, there may be more important things than development. An editor may want saleable topics; an engineer may want order and logic; a teacher may want style and good grammar. But for personal memoirs written for the family audience, nothing is more important than the details and images and sensations that permit one generation to share intimately with another.

As you begin to develop your material, there will be a nagging fear that you will bore your reader. If you just wipe out that fear and tell what you know you will achieve eighty percent of the development your writing needs. A mother keeping a journal on her young daughter says, "Do you expect me to write everything she does every day?" And the answer is, "Yes, and more—what she does and what you do to her and with her and for her, and how she feels and smells and sounds and tastes! Do not tell me that she is cute or that you love her. I will know that when you describe the warm odors of hair and scalp as your lips brush her ear." And I would add here, "Don't make it sound all sweetness and light in every entry. Include the incidents of exasperation and frustration and impatience. It is all part of the true fabric."

And I have heard older people, pleasantly surprised, ask, "You mean you *want* to know about *all* those things?" because when they have tried to speak of them, their audiences seemed not to care. And they are probably right. When I was younger, I was impatient with anyone who talked for more than three minutes. I could not tolerate chatter about the old homestead or Uncle Louie's job or Aunt Hazel running away from home. I closed my ears, and it is lost. Today I would be very grateful if I could read the details.

It is important to remember that writing is not speech. The speaker may ramble casually; the writer is orderly and purposeful. The speaker may grope for expression; the writer has revised and polished his or her style. The speaker may talk slowly; the written words come as quickly as the reader wants. When someone is talking too much, the audience has a hard time turning him or her off; if the writer goes into too much detail, the reader can skip to the next paragraph or page. Moreover, the speaker may have a captive and unwilling audience; the writer knows that the reader came to her or him out of a desire to discover and learn. And, finally, the speaker is talking to her or his contemporaries; the writer addresses both the near and the distant future.

So do not be afraid to write in detail. Develop; it is what your readers want. And don't doubt the value of all the things you observed and remember. They were important enough to impress you and implant themselves in your consciousness. Your special family audience will want to know them. Would you like to read the diary of one of

Caesar's legionnaires? Or a journal by Mary Magdalen? What details would you like to have omitted because they would bore you?

Do not tell me that Mary or the legionnaire are different. They were common people. History has made us see how special their experiences were. History and time will make your experiences special also.

Final Thoughts

Although your readers may have known some members of the family, they never knew them as you knew them. You knew them when they were younger and, perhaps, different in their attitudes, personalities, or experiences. For me, my grandfather was always an old man; for my father, he was middle-aged; for my great-uncle or for my great-grandfather, he was a boy. I wish someone had written about what my grandfather was like as a boy. But no one ever did or ever will.

That is, perhaps, the final guideline for developing material: Whatever you record survives; whatever you omit passes away. Future generations will read what you write, and you must think of them and what they will need and want to know about you and your experiences as you develop your writing.

When you write personal essays, memoirs, and family history, you are writing more for the future than for the present. You are creating a unique record of your experience of a particular historical time. Your future readers are blind, deaf, and numb to the times, peoples, and events of which you write. You are not only the eyes of the reader, you are the reader's ears, nose, skin, and very nerve endings. The reader is even mindless without you, wanting you to think and explain things. Nothing is obvious to the reader unless you make it so.

viii The Order of Things

If the topic is small and the development complete, then organization and coherence will be relatively easy.

I have read thousands of selections from memoirs and family histories, and organization is rarely a major problem. Therefore, I suspect that you need not worry much about organization in the rewriting of your material.

Compared to topic selection and development, which are often difficult to bring under control, organization is easy. If you have put the effort into working up a small, compact topic, then its individual organization is easier to grasp than is the organization of a broad, loose, complex group of life experiences.

If you have already written a rough draft and rewritten it once to improve the development, then you have already, consciously or unconsciously, done much of the organizing of the topic. Your logic, intuition, and basic feel for the material have probably taken you in the right direction.

In any event, for the type of writing we are talking about in this book, you may find it more practical to write a rough draft, letting the material flow onto the paper as the mind generates it, than to create a formal organization prior to the writing. For narratives in particular you need only a sense of where to start and where to end, because the time order is so clear.

There is no one correct way to organize a piece; there are always several equally effective organizations. In your first draft you may not have used the best organization, but you probably have avoided the worst. If what you have is readable and understandable, then we are concerned only with minor shifts and adjustments to improve a structure that is already eighty to ninety percent organized.

Transitional Words and Phrases to Improve Coherence

Your basic material may be in good order or sequence, but the connections between sentences or ideas may be vague or uncertain. If that's the case, the addition of appropriate transitional words or phrases may be all that is necessary to strengthen the coherence. Take the following example:

> Don and I bought the boat under the worst possible circumstances. We had never seen her before. We rowed out to her mooring late one night. She was no more than a dark silhouette against the night sky. We could make out her mast, but not the stays. We had a sense of her overall length, but not her lines or her color, or the condition of her hull. She heeled over sluggishly. The outboard rudder squeaked in complaint. We could smell the dampness and see the dark, oily bilge water as it sloshed over the floor-

boards. What we couldn't see was the rust-encrusted engine or the dry rot along the water line. She was a derelict, unused and uncared for. Don and I saw in her the stuff of our dreams—a twenty-eight-foot sailboat for a mere eight hundred dollars. We bought her on the spot.

The paragraph is disjointed in spots. The continuity and coherence are weak. Now read the same paragraph with a few key words and phrases added to improve the sense of relationship between ideas:

Don and I bought the boat under the worst possible circumstances. We had never seen her before *that night when* we rowed out to her mooring. *As we approached,* she was no more than a dark silhouette against the night sky. *Gradually* we could make out her mast, but not the stays. We had a sense of her overall length but not her lines or her color or the condition of her hull. *As we boarded her,* she heeled over sluggishly under our weight, *and* the outboard rudder squeaked in complaint. *When we opened the hatch into the cabin,* we could smell the dampness and see the dark, oily bilge water as it sloshed over the floorboards. What we couldn't see was the rust-encrusted engine or the dry rot along the water line. She was a derelict, unused and uncared for, *but because night shrouded much of her homely character,* Don and I saw in her the stuff of our dreams—a twenty-eight-foot sailboat for a mere eight hundred dollars! We bought her on the spot.

In the revised version we have not changed the sequence or order of information but merely strengthened the sense of relationship or connection between the ideas. Since this is a narrative sequence in which time relationships are important, we have used time-subordinated clauses like *when we rowed, as we boarded,* and *when we opened* to clarify the progression of events. The conjunction *and* in line 9 shows that those two events occurred at the same time and from the same cause. The adverb *gradually* tells how the view unfolded and reminds us that the view is still unfolding. The final conjunction and subordinate clause *but, because night shrouded* offers a qualifying reminder that helps us reconcile two apparently conflicting ideas, "She was a derelict" and "Don and I saw in her the stuff of our dreams."

If there is a logical order to the basic material, then the addition of select words and phrases during revision can improve the overall sense of coherence. Some of that revision may take you back into a reconsideration of basic sentence structure, a subject that is discussed in greater depth in the next chapter, but for our purposes here we can point out that short, simple sentences are sometimes choppy and disconnected because the proper coordinating and subordinating conjunctions are not present. Words like *and, or, nor, but, because, who, when, which, while, before,* and *after* are conjunctions that help clarify relationships between ideas. Using them to combine sentences or sentence elements will improve coherence.

Similarly, the conjunctive adverbs *so, thus, besides, hence, instead, however, therefore, nevertheless,* and *moreover* help the reader see relationships between statements. Phrases such as *on the other hand, of course, for example, in addition to,* and *with the exception of* also alert the reader.

And finally there are the formal structures—*first, second, third* or *A, B, C*—to indicate the steps or divisions in a topic.

The purpose of all such words and devices is to help the reader move smoothly and confidently through the material. A few such elements may be all you need to smooth out a paragraph or a composition.

Repetition to Improve Coherence

A more subtle sense of coherence and continuity is provided by the repetition of key words and phrases. In the previous sample *Don* and *I* and *the boat* and *the darkness* are key concepts. Notice that *Don* and *I* open the paragraph, and the two of us are echoed in the repetition of the pronoun *we* throughout. *Don and I* is restated in the conclusion to remind the reader to whom the *we* refers.

Boat is mentioned in the opening line and then referred to as *her* or *she. Derelict* becomes a synonym for the actual boat, while *stuff of our dreams—a twenty-eight foot sailboat . . .* is a counter point to *derelict.*

Repetition of key words, and the use of pronouns and synonyms which substitute for the key words, strengthen the sense of unity and coherence in the paragraph.

Organization

Recently a woman asked, "How am I going to get all my ideas organized? I have so much to say, and I don't know where to start."

The answer is, "You don't have to get it *all* organized. And you can start almost anywhere."

Let's go back to one of our basic premises: You should be writing short pieces of a few thousand words on simple, limited topics. Instead of trying to "organize" ten or twenty or fifty years of experience and observation, choose a small, carefully focused topic and concentrate on telling or explaining that topic. *Organization is only the sequence in which you decide to tell or explain.* Like a road map, it's good if it gets us where we are supposed to go; it's no good if we get lost.

The woman I mentioned before said, "Well, my children would like for me to write what it was like during the Great Depression. But I don't know where to start;

there's just so much to say! I've told them about the hard times and all the hardships we went through in those days." And then almost immediately she added, "I remember in 1933 having to travel from South Carolina to Georgia, where my husband's family lived. My husband hadn't had a job for months, and we had only six dollars —just enough for me and the baby to take the bus; my husband was going to hitch hike. That baby fussed all the time, the poor, sickly little thing. I'm sure the other people on the bus wished us gone. And I had to walk in on my in-laws, people I'd never met, without a penny to my name, no husband, and a howling baby. And my poor husband—it took him nearly two weeks to get there. I don't know how he made it at all with no money for food or nothing."

The answer to her problem is obvious. She should start with that incident—it is sharp and clear in her mind, she feels strongly about it, and it is small enough and self-contained enough to be covered in six or eight pages. Basically all she needs to do is provide a paragraph or two of introduction or background and then tell us about the decision to go to Georgia, buying the ticket, saying good-bye to her husband, then telling us what it was like on the bus, how she felt, and what happened on her arrival at the home of her in-laws. *Since it is essentially a story or narrative, she should tell about her experience in the sequence in which things happened.* Her sixty-second summation is her outline.

Several people in the workshop, having heard her brief summary, said, "Why don't you just write about that?"

Her reply was, "Can I do that? I thought I would have to start at the beginning."

But what is the beginning? When the baby was born? When the husband lost his job six months earlier? When they were married? When the stock market crashed in 1929? When she left school? When she was born? If we look at the broad sweep and variety of our lives, of course it seems impossible to organize and write. The task is overwhelming. But if we can say, "Here is an *incident* that stands out in my mind and that says something about my life," then we can start right there.

Notice that we need very little background to get into her story. Even the brief information I have given you here is enough for us to grasp the basics of the situation. We would like to read the special details of her experience and observation so that we can see it more clearly, *but the order seems almost obvious.*

In the same way most of your material is likely to have an obvious order or sequence, and for that reason overall organization should not present much of a problem for you or your readers. But if you have a topic that just won't take shape, then read on; maybe some conventional forms will help.

Paragraphing: The Key to Organization

I have a friend, a writer, who says, "Organization is no trouble for me. Every story has a beginning, a middle, and an end. All you have to do is figure out which part is which so you know what goes first." That's the subjective and intuitive approach. When it's working, you don't need much else. When it's not working, you need an objective guide to the conventional patterns of organization.

An objective approach to the problem of organization requires us to look at the paragraph, because what we call organization is either (1) a question of the internal arrangement of sentences within the paragraph or (2) a question of the order in which the paragraphs occur. We will look first at the internal arrangement of paragraphs and second at the overall organization of paragraphs as might be reflected in an outline. In reviewing some of the basic elements in paragraph structure and arrangement, you may get some ideas on how to organize or reorganize your material.

But it is important to remember that principles of paragraphing are not rules; at most they are guidelines or reminders to help you over rough spots. It may help to understand types of paragraphs, but each paragraph you write is unique and especially suited to you, your message, and your audience. I have said before that writing is mostly a matter of judgment; it involves a sense or feel for audience, language, concept, and purpose. Some of the ideas and suggestions here may help improve your judgment or your way of seeing your own writing, but in no way should you abandon your sense of language and depend upon dry, mechanical rules and forms. After all, the writing should reflect your personality, and it can't do that if your judgment is not in control.

Nowhere is personal voice more important than in the memoir or family history. I had a clear demonstration of this while working with an American Indian who was writing about an event he had witnessed on the Flathead Reservation in Montana. His story had strong character, dramatic conflict, and vivid details in an interesting setting. At the center of action was a game at which two men were gambling.

After reading his piece I made some suggestions on reorganizing the paragraphs. He made a few changes and handed it back to me. Most of my suggestions had been ignored. So I took the first few pages and rewrote them and reorganized them; I added a few "vigorous" verbs to punch up the style and gave it back to him, saying, "This is what I mean. It would be clearer if you wrote it this way." His response was, "I see what you mean. But Indians don't think that way or talk that way. An Indian wouldn't use a verb like *slither*. This is not the Indian way."

And he was absolutely right! I was dead wrong in trying

to impose my Anglo-Saxon patterns on his material. My version might have been clearer for an Anglo audience, but it would have lacked his personal "voice" and uniqueness. Fortunately, he had enough confidence in his sense of self and purpose and his sense of audience to resist my "conventional" forms.

As we move in this chapter and the next into a discussion of form and style, it is important to remember that these are abstract principles and guidelines; they represent convention, or the norm. As a result, they are impersonal. Use whatever you can and don't worry about the rest. Don't substitute dry, mechanical forms that are stiff and unfamiliar for the natural, easy flow of your personal style.

If you have doubts about your skills as a writer—and almost everyone does—don't let those doubts overwhelm your judgment. Don't abandon your present writing style for every new piece of advice you read. Consider it and assimilate it gradually, a sentence or paragraph at a time. If it works and feels right, keep it. If not, forget it. Don't expect magic. There are no sudden cures or high-technology innovations. Your writing should reflect who and what you are, and you should no more expect sudden changes in your writing than you should expect sudden changes in your personality. In most cases your judgment and resulting style of writing will change gradually as you gain writing experience and command of your material. Let it happen gradually, naturally.

Types of Paragraphs

In the tradition of beginning, middle, and end, the types of paragraphs are:

introductory paragraphs
body paragraphs

expository
descriptive
narrative
dialogue
transitional
specialized forms
concluding paragraphs

These paragraphs differ in function and in form, but remember that all the functions and forms attempt to bring the readers into the material, to help them understand it and share in the experience, and then to conclude it for them. Paragraphs are structural arrangements, webs or bridges designed by the writer to lead the audience through a series of mental steps or sensory perceptions or a sequence of action events.

Introductory paragraphs. The introduction can be as simple or as complex as you think necessary. Here is the way Carl Cleveland began the piece "Granddad's Jackknife":

> Man, for all his ingenuity, has never perfected a tool of greater simplicity and at the same time utility and versatility than Granddad's jackknife.
>
> It seems to me a mark of decadence that few men today carry a jackknife, or for that matter a knife of any kind. Granddad would have felt but half-dressed without his knife in his pocket.
>
> With its plain bone handle, the knife. . . .

This is a simple, direct introduction. It establishes two basic but related ideas, one about the knife—its utility and versatility—and one about Granddad and how he would have felt half-dressed without his knife. After that the body of the piece begins with a detailed description of the specific knife. The whole introduction takes three sentences. Limited, simple topics usually require no more than a paragraph or two of introduction.

The most common introductory paragraph is the "inverted pyramid," which starts broadly with a few sentences establishing a time, place, or general context and then focuses on the specific, limited topic to be discussed. For example, Carl Cleveland moves from *man* and *knife* in the abstract to *Granddad* and his specific pocketknife. Once again, the questions *who, what, when,* and *where* can be used to help orient the reader to the topic that is about to be introduced. The inverted-pyramid form favors the broad establishing statements first and the specific statement of topic or thesis—the "point"—as the last sentence in the introductory paragraph. Here is an example:

> There are people for whom guns represent violence, but for me growing up in the thirties and forties in rural and small-town environments, guns were a very natural part of my life. My relatives, both male and female, used rifles and shotguns for hunting. As a kid, I owned cap guns, water guns, dart guns that fired sticks with suction cups, BB guns, a .22 rifle and a shotgun. In my experience it was only the rubber gun that had the stigma of violence attached to it.

This introductory paragraph sets up a time and place and context. It talks about guns and violence and the types of guns I owned and comes to focus on the rubber gun. With the last sentence in the introduction—my thesis sentence—the reader has been guided to the specific topic I want to write about. That thesis sentence is my *entrée.* I must now move to the body and an explanation of what a rubber gun is, how it was used, and why it had the stigma of violence associated with it.

Whether you call it an inverted pyramid or whether you think of it as a funnel, such introductory paragraphs

—broad at the top and narrowing to a "point" at the bottom—are good beginnings. Audiences are usually more comfortable with and receptive to an idea if they are prepared for it. Often our whole sense of relevancy and meaning depends upon having a context or frame of reference in which to fit the writer's message.

There is a difference between introductory paragraphs and "openings." In a sense the title of your piece is an opening; it is the reader's first clue to the topic of discussion and perhaps to the tone or mood. "Granddad's Jackknife" gives the reader a pretty clear idea of the writer's topic. For our purposes, let your title reveal clearly what it is you are writing about.

An opening paragraph, as opposed to an introductory paragraph, might read something like this "narrative lead":

> The London cab was out of its element, straining along at forty-six miles per hour on the Norfolk plains, its chain drive complaining, its driver lost and confused in the predawn darkness and swirling snow. In the unheated passenger compartment four airmen hunched together in shivering, fitful sleep.

If this opening works it has aroused the audience's interest and curiosity. They want to know what is going on and what happens next. Because there is no thesis sentence or revelation of topic, the audience doesn't know what it's all about, but curiosity motivates them to read on.

That type of lead or "hook" may be familiar to you from magazines and books, where it is used to capture the reader's attention and thereby attract potential buyers. It's invaluable to the commercial writer in the commercial market, *but it's not necessary for the family audience.*

Similarly, other appeals and hooks and leads and special openings may be interesting and inventive devices, but their primary purpose is to intrigue and motivate the audience to read what follows. However, the family audience doesn't have to be motivated. We've assumed they come with built-in interest in family stories and history. They need only an adequate *orientation,* which is the purpose of the conventional introductory paragraph with its thesis sentence. Keep it plain and simple, direct and clear.

Concluding paragraphs. Conclusions are natural companions to introductions—they are often no more than echoes. The simplest and perhaps most common conclusion is one that restates the ideas or sentiments contained in the introduction. For example, my rubber-gun piece might end this way:

> So our rubber guns, which began as simple toys, ended as weapons of violence.

This is no more than a one-sentence restatement of the thesis sentence expressed at the end of my introductory paragraph. Such a simple restatement is often all that is required by way of a conclusion.

A conclusion with more elaboration and extension on the thesis might read like this:

> So our rubber guns, which began as simple toys, ended as weapons of violence. In that final battle we learned our lesson: Bigger guns begat still bigger guns. Greater violence begat yet greater violence. The giving and receiving of pain wasn't much fun. By mutual accord we simply quit. With childlike clarity we opted for more pleasant forms of competition, and the rubber guns fell into disfavor and disuse. I never made another after that day.

In such a conclusion I provide more interpretation and explanation for my readers. In terms of clarity such an extended conclusion will ensure that my readers get the meaning I want them to have. There is some moralizing or philosophizing in such a conclusion, but there is nothing wrong with that. If experience has taught you a lesson or a moral principle, why not pass it on to your descendants? Why not transmit to them your thinking, wisdom, insight, and understanding, your philosophy or morality? After all, it's what you are, and that is what the memoir should reflect.

Often there is a balance between introduction and conclusion, a sort of going out by the way in as well as a return to the theme and ideas in the opening paragraph. But you may think of your conclusion simply as "closure," and it can be very informal. Carl Cleveland, for example, concludes his catalog of knife uses with his grandfather and some other men talking politics and whittling away. His last few lines read:

> It seems to me a basic element missing from politics today is whittling. Maybe if more men carried jackknives and knew how to use them, our elections might be more meaningful.

I used *closure* as opposed to a *formal conclusion* in the piece on my grandfather's wooden leg. I assumed that my readers had some sense of how my grandfather felt about his leg after I had discussed it for several pages. After quoting the last line of the last incident when the woman asks, "Is Mr. Hofmann ill?" I closed with, "Grandpa would have loved that." It *suggests* Grandpa's attitude.

In that kind of closure I leave summation and interpretation up to the reader. The closure is minimal—and it is a gamble. I gamble that my portrait of Grandfather is clear enough to be understood without a formal conclusion. If I'm wrong—if I lose the gamble—then my readers will not understand all that I want them to understand. It's a matter of judgment, which improves with practice but is always fallible.

The introductory and concluding paragraphs, unlike the body paragraphs, are often general rather than specific; they are often summary in nature, given to broader overviews. Their purpose is to connect and disconnect, to say hello and good-bye; they tell the reader where the body will go and where the body has been. Introductions and conclusions do not tell stories in detail; the body does that. The introduction prepares the readers for what is to come or gets them in the proper mood or frame of mind. The conclusion tells them that it is over and perhaps tells them what it all means in a few quick sentences. But the best introductions and conclusions are nothing without the body. After all, at this point you still don't know what really happened back in the days when I was making rubber guns.

The body paragraph. We are talking here about five different types of paragraphs, each with its own internal logic and structure:

> expository paragraphs
> descriptive paragraphs
> narrative paragraphs
> dialogue paragraphs
> transitional paragraphs

There is a sixth category I've called specialized forms, which are discussed briefly at the end of this section.

It is sometimes difficult to tell expository, descriptive, and narrative paragraphs apart. They are often intermingled, and they do not always exist in pure forms. But for our purposes you can think of expository paragraphs as those that explain an interpretation or intellectual concept; descriptive paragraphs as those that report sensory data on the physical world; and narrative paragraphs as those that emphasize character action performed in a time sequence.

EXPOSITORY PARAGRAPHS.

The expository paragraph explains an idea or a process. It is often said to have the same form as an essay or an article; that is, it has an introduction, a body, and a conclusion. In practice the expository paragraph may have a topic or an introductory sentence; it certainly will contain anywhere from five to fifteen or more sentences of details, facts, examples, definitions, and images to explain its concept. It may or may not have a conclusion. What follows is an example of a typical expository paragraph that explains a process:

When he built a turkey blind, my uncle was always careful of its location, depth, and concealment. He would first pick a location forty or fifty yards inside a stand of live oak trees. Usually the terrain was level to permit maximum viewing on all sides. Then he would begin by digging a pit, much like a foxhole, about four feet deep and six feet in diameter, in the sandy soil. As he dug, he would pile the sand in a neat ring around the perimeter of the pit so that it had a raised collar or shoulder. When the pit was finished, he would trim branches from the surrounding live oaks and arrange them in a tight, interlocking circle on top of the ridge of dirt around the pit. He might also incorporate other shrubs and plants into the live oak branches as he cleared brush from his field of vision. On occasion he would line the inside surface of the branches with old burlap sacks. He could see through the loose weave of burlap, but the turkeys couldn't see him. He always built the blinds months ahead of when he planned to use them, so the turkeys would get used to them. He was a cagey and game-wise hunter, and his blinds were so natural in their setting that I often walked upon one before

I realized what it was. And, of course, that was the final test: The game warden shouldn't be able to spot it, either.

The major difference between this expository paragraph on building a turkey blind and a descriptive or narrative paragraph on the same subject is slight. This is expository because I have abstracted and standardized the *process,* made it seem universal. By a mental act I have combined my observations and created a "typical" blind. It's not one specific blind but a synthesis of many.

A description of an *individual* turkey blind might describe the colors of the soil and branches, the sounds in the woods, the stillness in the air, the grit of sand between the fingers, and so on. The emphasis in a descriptive paragraph would be more on *sensation* relating to a specific object, place, and time.

A narrative would be a more immediate *story,* in which my uncle would be more strongly present as a person, and his actions and perhaps his words or thoughts might be communicated to the reader. If he stopped to rest or drink or eat or smoke, that might be part of the narrative, but it is not a necessary part of the process of building a turkey blind.

The differences are slight, but real. And it helps in the organization of material to know our purpose—do we want to explain a somewhat generalized or abstracted process; do we want to describe a specific person, place, or thing; or do we want to narrate a specific line of action, re-creating scenes in the simulation of real life?

The organization of an expository paragraph, because it deals with abstractions, mental processes, and thought, is likely to favor "logical" patterns and sequences. For example, the steps of site selection, excavation, and concealment in the turkey-blind paragraph represent a logical sequence that follows time order because processes are steps in time. Almost every explanation of a process is likely to follow a time and/or causation order.

However, I could approach a subject like the turkey blind and express a concept such as:

> Concealment is the most important function of a good turkey blind. The pit must be deep enough so the hunter can sit or squat comfortably for hours without his head showing above the perimeter of brush. The brush and other parts of the enclosure, such as burlap, should obscure his presence and movement while still permitting the hunter to see through the screening to view the game. The position of the pit in the terrain should be such that . . .

In such a paragraph I have abstracted the topic—concealment—and organized it by beginning in the pit, moving logically and consistently to the perimeter of brush, then to the field of vision, and I could go on to describe the forest setting. That is a logical sequence, given my purpose and starting point.

Similarly, I could begin far outside the woods and move in to the perimeter and then in to the pit. That would also be a logical sequence. Because the mind can abstract and restructure experience and even create new concepts, its patterns of order are almost limitless. What is important for the writer is to understand the logic of his or her thought sequence and to present the ideas in an order that clearly explains the thinking to the reader.

But while the order of individual sentences is dictated by the thinking of the writer, the most common pattern of organization in expository paragraphs is a topic sentence that states the point of the paragraph, followed by step-by-step explanations in a "logical" order, perhaps ending with a summary, evaluation, or interpretation.

Thus a knowledge of form helps the writer organize his or her thoughts and expressions.

If the purpose of the expository paragraph is to make the reader think or understand, then the purpose of the descriptive paragraph is to make the reader see, hear, feel, taste, or smell. The following selection refers to most of the senses:

Sunday in the Barracks

The barracks were large, rectangular, two-story wooden boxes. At each end of the barracks, on the lower bay, were double doors, constantly open in summer to let the breezes in. On the upper bay there was one double door to the fire escape outside, and at the other end there was a stairwell to the floor below. The breezes flowed cool and gentle through the doors, down the center aisles of each bay, between the two-tiered rows of bunks, whispering sometimes through the bunks and out the open windows behind them.

On each bunk the rough wool khaki blankets stretched tautly across the light bow of mattress and shallow arch of pillow. At the foot of each bed along the center aisle hung the olive drab musette bags, and beneath them the olive drab footlockers. At the head of the beds along the wall hung the bulging olive drab duffel bags, and at intervals between the bunks were the olive drab wall lockers. On Sundays the new recruits in olive drab fatigues and undershirts rested quietly among the bunks and lockers, writing letters home. The wood barracks, like orchard trees, had seen many seasons of olive men and gear.

The sun-bleached breeze sneaking indoors soaked up the odor of new clothing and canvas and twill, of shoe polish and blitz rags and the alkaline yellow GI soap with which the bare timbers of the bay floors had been scrubbed. For the letter writers there was the faintest odor of new paper or ink, and the thick taste of mucilage on the tongue.

If there was a burst of energy among some of the young men, their first thought was to leave the barracks quickly, honoring the meditations of the letter writers. Thus the talking and scuffling spilled outdoors and spent itself in sports or bull sessions on the steps, and the silence inside was left intact.

In description, as in most other writing, the writer has to be more orderly than life or nature. The senses receive information from many directions simultaneously, but the writer must present a sense of order to his or her descriptive information. In the previous example the movement is from the overall barracks to the two bays, upper and lower, and the doors on each bay and the breezes coming through the doors, down the aisles, around the bunks, and out the windows. Then the bunks are visually described, first overall, then head to foot.

Such order is typical of description because it is roughly *spatial*. The mind's eye scans the building, then the floors, then the aisles, then the bunks, and then the objects around the bunks. Within that general spatial order there is the unity of senses: first what is seen and felt, then smelled and tasted, and, finally, heard. Order and unity work together to create coherence.

NARRATIVE PARAGRAPHS.

If description deals with sensory details, then narration deals with action. Narrative writing is storytelling, the report of events as they unfold. The most common order for narrative writing is straightforward time sequence, from start to finish. There are options for inverted time orders, flashbacks, overlapping sequences, or multiple perspectives in parallel time, but for memoirs and family history the simpler forms are preferable because they are easier to write and easier to read and understand.

The time order or *chronological sequence* in narration is so common that it is rarely a problem. From a very early age we learn to narrate our experiences in the sequences in which they occur. In an individual narrative paragraph we are not likely to have someone slamming a door before he goes out or drinking a cup of coffee before it is poured. We don't dry ourselves before we take a shower, and we don't put on our shoes and then our socks. Familiar life patterns and familiar events don't pose organizational problems.

The problem in narration sometimes occurs not in the individual paragraph but within the overall structure of the story. For example, I may want to tell you about my daughter Kathlyn and the time she fell off a log bridge and into a cold stream. Certain elements are important to your understanding of the story, so I must establish the location, the time of year, and her age—she was about seven. If I don't report her age early enough in the sequence, the reader will not know the type of person I am talking about. If I don't establish that there is a stream under the log bridge, the reader will be surprised when I report that she fell into it. It is the establishment of such details that is critical to the readers' understanding. Placing key details in the right place is the most common organizational problem in narration.

DIALOGUE PARAGRAPHS.

Dialogue is one of the best ways to represent a person, because it lets the person speak directly to the reader. In personality profiles, in biographical sketches, in narrative incidents, and even in autobiographical statements, quoted speech is immediate, revealing, and stimulating.

Unfortunately, writers often avoid dialogue because they are unfamiliar with its forms and conventions. But learning its few rules is worth the trouble. Nothing can bring a personality or an incident to life quite as dialogue can. Here are some basic guidelines for dialogue paragraphs:

1. The purpose of dialogue is to *approximate* speech, to create the illusion of reality, not to reproduce every word and cough. Be sparing with colloquialisms, speech abnormalities, phonetic spellings, and the like. You want to capture the flavor of a speaker's idiom and style but not every nuance, slur, and sibilant.

2. Indent and start a new paragraph with each change of speaker.

3. Enclose the spoken words in double quotation marks: "Thank you."

4. On the rare occasions when you have a quotation within a quotation, use the double quotation marks on the "outside" to enclose everything the speaker utters. Use the single quotation marks on the 'inside' to enclose quoted words the speaker is repeating: Momma answered, "Your father has said many times, 'Jake Sauer doesn't set foot in this house.' "

5. Where a speech is long, running to several paragraphs without interruption, place quotation marks at the beginning of each paragraph to remind the readers that they are still reading speech. Use the closing quotation marks only at the end of the speech, not at the end of each paragraph.

6. Identify the speaker clearly and directly with the conventional referrants: *I said, she said, Helen said.* Don't try for variety to avoid repetition. The vari-

ety quickly becomes more of problem than the routine it tries to cure. Readers are not bothered or bored by referrants that identify speakers clearly and directly. But if you write in every other line of dialogue, *"Helen coughed . . . spat . . . sneered . . . snarled . . . laughed . . . cried . . . whispered . . . shouted . . . sighed . . . lamented . . . bemoaned . . . complained. . . . "* before long the reader will begin to wonder if Helen really is consumptive, angry, sad, or paranoid-schizophrenic, or if the writer is forcing the material to satisfy a misguided desire for variety. Simplicity and moderation are the best guidelines.

7. In the same vein, avoid excess adverb modifiers: *". . . he said carefully . . . logically . . . sweetly . . . angrily . . . softly. . . . "* As in the Tom Swift tradition, this quickly becomes obvious and comic.

8. Don't have your speakers constantly addressing one another by their names just to keep the reader clear about who is speaking. Addressing another person by his or her name or title is common only on meeting and parting, in highly formal situations, for special emphasis to alert someone, to focus the voice on one person in a group, or to call someone who is distant or out of sight.

9. Other narrative, descriptive, and expository statements may precede or follow the spoken words in the same paragraph.

Basic Examples:

1) Grandma said, "Run out to the garden and pick me some fresh okra."

2) "Run out to the garden," said Grandma, "and pick me some fresh okra."

3) "Run out to the garden and pick me some fresh okra," Grandma said. "Don't take all afternoon either."

NOTE: Position of the referrant is a matter of author choice. It may be varied for purposes of clarity, emphasis, continuity, variety, or rhythm.

NOTE: In example 2 the words, *said Grandma,* interrupt the sentence, and, like other interruptors, are set off with commas. The words that follow the interruption are not a new sentence; therefore the first letter in the word *and* is not capitalized. Example 3 shows how to punctuate and capitalize when one sentence ends with a referrant, and a new sentence of dialogue continues.

NOTE: In these examples, all punctuation, except for that immediately following the word *said,* is enclosed within the quotation marks.

4) "You want some tomatoes, too?" I asked.

NOTE: If the spoken words form a question, the question mark is placed within the quotation marks.

The notation for dialogue is logical and consistent. After you practice it for a page or two and then review your notation, you will find that the writing and punctuating of dialogue become easier and more automatic. Within a short time it will be as natural as your other patterns of sentence and paragraph design, and it will provide a special flavor to your writing.

TRANSITIONAL PARAGRAPHS.

We discussed transitional words and phrases earlier in this chapter. Transitional paragraphs are simply an extension of those shorter forms. Whereas transitional words and phrases tie sentences and paragraphs together, transitional paragraphs bridge major divisions in a story, an article, or an essay.

If you have a story in which there is a significant time lapse between events, you might write a short transitional paragraph to bridge that time interval. If you can imagine a section of story dealing with how we hauled water during a drought—where we got it, how we hauled it, how far, and so on—and then a following section about the new windmill and how it worked and changed things, then the problem becomes: how can we make the transition from the account on hauling water to the second account of the new windmill? A short transitional paragraph is the answer:

> . . . Then the men would open the tailgate of the pickup and, one by one, move the barrels to the tailgate platform, tip them over, and spill the water into the troughs. Then they loaded them and started all over again.
>
> Things went on that way for another three months. Hauling water simply became a part of the farm routine while we waited for the new well to be completed.
>
> Finally, in late September, with everything parched and dry and the cattle bawling for water, all the well casing was in place, and the windmill tower was. . . .

The sample here provides for a time lapse of three months. In a similar fashion, if there is a significant shift in location, in subject matter, or in ideas, the reader often needs a little help to make that shift. The transitional paragraph does the job. It is usually short and often summary in nature. It doesn't have the development and structure of a standard expository paragraph or a descriptive paragraph. In some ways it is closer to the introductory and the concluding paragraphs: They get the reader in and out of the whole composition; the transitional paragraph gets the reader out of one section and into another.

In most cases the transitions required in short, simple narratives and reports can be taken care of with phrases and sentences. Transitional paragraphs are rare in short articles and essays.

SPECIALIZED FORMS OF THE PARAGRAPH.

These are not units of discussion or speech, as are the other paragraphs. These are paragraphs only because they have been indented and set off like paragraphs.

For example, an author may want special emphasis for a one-sentence or one-word statement. So he spaces and indents it as a separate paragraph. Setting it off that way gives it emphasis. You will see this type of paragraphing most commonly in advertising and promotional literature.

Another type of specialized paragraph form is the journalistic paragraph. Newspapers, magazines, and journals that print their material in narrow columns require frequent paragraph breaks even when the logic of paragraphing as we have discussed it here does not require a new paragraph.

Look at your local newspaper. Chances are that most paragraphs are less than three sentences in length. This is partially the result of writing easily readable prose for a mass audience and partially the result of breaking up blocks of type to make it seem less formidable. The paragraphing in Carl Cleveland's essay on his grandfather's pocketknife is the result of journalistic choices; his piece was paragraphed that way by the editor or composer when it was printed in the Seattle *Times Sunday Magazine* supplement.

For further examples compare the paragraphing in a local or regional paper with the paragraphing in national newspapers like the *Wall Street Journal* or the *Christian Science Monitor,* which are published for a more select audience. Those differences point up an important qualification about all paragraphing: While there is a "textbook" form for paragraphs, many paragraphs do not follow those rules and guidelines. Paragraphing, like other literary forms and conventions, can be altered to suit the needs of the audience or the objectives of the author. It remains a matter of judgment.

Outlining

By now you should have an ever-expanding list of topics. That list is a primitive outline, a sketchy, informal guide to future writing projects. The writing program for your annual publication which we discussed in chapter II is an outline. Outlines are everywhere, and you use them constantly to organize your activities. But in all cases the purpose of the outline is the same: It helps us keep track of what we are supposed to do.

My father used to talk about an old German carpenter he worked with. They were installing the rafters and trusses for the roof on a house, and there were some complicated angles and pitches involved where three or four roof planes came together in one spot. The foreman was measuring to determine the angles of cut and the length of the boards, trying to figure out the complicated geometry. The old German kept sawing and hammering away and solved the problem in his head and had the job done before the foreman had finished his "outline."

Writing is a little bit that way. If you know your craft and your material, if your experience and habits and intuition and native talents let you write without an outline, then do so. On the other hand, if you are still learning or if you are uncertain or unfamiliar with your material, then outlining may be the most efficient and dependable approach to solving the problem.

OUTLINE PROCEDURES AND FORMATS.

On the simplest level, the outline is nothing but a list. It indicates *what* topics to write about, but not the order in which they should occur, nor their relative size, complexity, or level of importance.

Step One: Choose a topic from the writing list.

Step Two: Break it down into different sub-topics of discussion. Don't worry about the order.

EXAMPLE:

Topic: Uncle Tom Birchfield

Breakdown:
  Family branch
  physical appearance
  palsey
  stoop
  personality
  dress
  work
  speech
  sense of humor
  relationship with others

Step Three: Subdivide further and indicate major versus minor points. Group and order elements. Begin use of standard number/letter notation.

  I. Place in the family.
  II. Early health problems affected physical appearance.
      A. Height, weight, and bearing.
      B. Dress.
      C. Speech.
      D. Palsey.
  III. Personality.
      A. Sense of humor.
          1. How he laughed.
          2. Things he did.

  B. Attitude toward work.

  C. His temper and irritability.

  D. Prejudices.

 IV. Relationship with others.

  A. His brother, Irl.

  B. His mother.

  C. My mother and me.

NOTE: The outline at this point does not have an "introduction" or a "conclusion." At this stage, the objective is to specify the details and organization and patterns of subordination within the "body" of the piece.

A second or even third version of this topic outline might be necessary before proceeding to a *sentence* outline. For complex or unfamiliar subjects, the sentence outline is the most dependable and efficient form of outlining; it forces the writer to express his or her thoughts in complete sentences. For the first time, the writer's vague ideas must take a definitive shape.

Usually, the sentence outline begins with a formal thesis sentence or statement of purpose. It then follows the conventional outline format and notation, except that *all* entries in the outline are written as complete sentences. The following example is just the beginning of a sentence outline on the topic of Uncle Tom. Notice how some of the ideas take on a totally different dimension when expressed in complete sentences:

Step Four: Translate topic headings into sentences. Thesis Statement: Uncle Tom was perhaps the most unfortunate and unlikable member of my family, because, either for reasons of health or innate meanness, he was often troublesome, mean, and selfish.

  I. My mother's brother, christened Thomas Jefferson Birchfield, was born in Vernon, Texas, in 1900, the third of six children born to Francis Marion Birchfield and Mary Elvira (née Russell) Birchfield.

II. During his teens he contracted what the family always referred to as "sleeping sickness," probably a form of encephalitis, which affected him for the rest of his life.

    A. When I knew him in the 1930s the most obvious result of his disease was an overall lethargy.

        1. He was about six feet one inch tall, the tallest member of the family.

        2. He had long arms which hung limply at his sides.

        3. He was of a heavy, fleshy build, weighing about 240 pounds.

        4. He walked slowly, usually scuffing his feet, as though lifting them or bending the knee required too much effort.

        5. Most of his other movements tended to be slow and poorly coordinated.

            a. Removing his hat and hanging it on a peg could take a full half-minute.

            b. Climbing into the pickup and shutting the door was an agonizing slow-motion sequence.

    B. He always wore heavy black

work shoes, dark gray baggy pants that hung low on his hips, a nondescript gray or blue shirt, and a battered felt hat.

C. His speech was slow, even by southern standards.

D. He was sometimes seized by a palsied, violent shaking of his right hand.

    1. The most violent shaking seemed to occur when we were all seated at the dining table.

        a. The very first time I witnessed him violently shaking his knife against the plate, it frightened me.

           1) There was a fierce clatter of metal against porcelain.

           2) The whole table vibrated.

        b. Such events occurred three or four times during a meal—often, said his brother, Irl, when he was being ignored or when he was losing an argument.

    2. The palsey did affect him at other times when he was performing small manual chores, but it was much less severe.

III. I am not sure of all the physical and

psychological things that shaped his personality, but the end product was unpleasant.

A. He had a vicious sense of humor.
  1.————————————
  2.————————————
B. ————————————

NOTE: Even at this stage of development the outline could undergo further changes. For example, entries II. B. and II. C. interrupt the description of his physical movements. II. A.5. deals with hand movements and so does II. D.1. and 2. They should probably be grouped together.

A sentence outline forces the writer to organize and develop his thoughts much more completely than does a topical or fragmentary outline. The sentence outline takes extra time to prepare, but it can be time well spent. It may make the writing of the rough draft easier, because the sentence outline forces memory and conceptualization and suggests both topic sentences and illustrations that will develop those paragraphs. In number of words and sentences, a comprehensive sentence outline may equal ten to twenty percent of the final paper.

For long and complex topics that may require months to write, the detailed sentence outline provides a more stable plan of attack than would a sketchy outline. For example, when I was beginning work on this book, I spent over three months developing ever more detailed sentence outlines. The final outline I submitted to the publisher ran to forty pages. It was a year after the submission of the outline before I began to put the whole manuscript together. But that outline was a constant aid as I navigated through this material. It didn't anticipate everything that went down on the pages, but it kept bringing me back on course and kept reminding me of ideas and examples that should be included in each chapter.

It was not the *book* outline that was so important, but rather the *chapter* outlines that provided the best guides. With your own work it is not the outline of your life or of the family members that is important but rather the outlines of individual events and individual biographical sketches that are important. In this example about my Uncle Tom, I outlined only one of a dozen biographical sketches dealing with my mother's family. More importantly, this is only one of several pieces dealing with my Uncle Tom. The old premise still applies: *Keep the topics small and simple.* The outline should open up and discover the internal richness of the topic, but the topic itself remains narrow and focused.

Five to ten such topics will make an annual magazine; five to ten magazines will make a book. That's the way books are made—a paragraph at a time, a topic at a time, a chapter or a section at a time. It grows. No one writes books—one writes sentences that become paragraphs that become chapters that become books.

For some writers and for some topics, outlining will be a great help. For others it will seem stiff and artificial. For many people the quick, rough draft remains the better way to approach writing topics. The rough draft with its natural, easy flow is also a kind of outline; it is an intermediate expression, an approximation of the final statement. It usually requires revision, but so does the essay or article written from an outline. There is no magic and no right way. The means, the conventional forms and devices, should not become ends in themselves. The true objective remains the communication of family life to the family audience, by whatever method. Silence remains the only real failure.

ix The
Last Time Around

Only when you are satisfied with the basic content and organization of your writing should you concern yourself with the issues of style, grammar, punctuation, and spelling.

There comes a time when every writer says, "It may not be perfect, but I've done the best I can." That may occur after one revision or after several—writers work in different ways. But when you reach that point, it is better for you to go on to another topic than to struggle uncertainly with additional changes. No piece of writing is ever perfect, and no writer is ever totally satisfied.

In the final phase of revision, there are a few hard-and-fast rules to be observed and a lot of gray area, especially where older formal conventions have given way to casual and informal usage. Beyond the gray area is an infinite domain of choices dictated by the individual style and esthetic of each writer.

The hard-and-fast rules are probably the most familiar and offer the fewest problems: Sentences begin with capital letters and end with periods, question marks, or exclamation points. Plural subjects take plural verbs. Or, *i* before *e* except after *c,* or when sounded as *ay* as in *neighbor* and *weigh.* You probably follow such standard rules and conventions automatically.

The gray areas are where there are exceptions to the rules, where traditions are changing, or where several choices exist. Spelling rules on when to and when not to double a final consonant when adding *ed* confuse many. The use of *who* and *whom* created so much confusion that *whom* has now almost disappeared from informal usage. Commas come and go—mostly go—and the exceptions for their placement could fill a chapter in a handbook. Differences in expression, syntax, diction, and punctuation are often a matter of judgment, not always clearly right or wrong. When it comes to style, esthetics, and individual preference, then subjectivity, intuition, and personal taste reign. Each writer steers his or her own course within very broad limits.

Sentence Patterns and Punctuation: Problem Areas

FRAGMENTS.

Fragments are incomplete sentences and thus are incomplete thoughts. They result, usually, from one of two things: (1) the verb has been omitted accidentally from the sentence; or, (2) key elements have been subordinated without providing a main clause.

INCORRECT: George and Millie's first car with its large headlights and fat, white-sidewall tires mounted on steel spoke rims. (No verb for the subject, *car.*)

REVISED: George and Millie's first car *had* large headlights and fat, white-sidewall tires mounted on steel spoke rims.

RUN-ON SENTENCES.

The problem here is two sentences, usually closely related, which are run together as one sentence, without benefit of punctuation or conjunction.

INCORRECT: My father and my brother dug the well it took them three weeks.

REVISED: My father and my brother dug the well; it took them three weeks.

OR.......   My father and my brother dug the well. It took them three weeks.

OR.......   My father and my brother dug the well in three weeks.

OR.......   My father and my brother dug the well, but it took them three weeks.

COMMA SPLICES OR COMMA FAULTS.

These result when the writer recognizes a run-on problem and splices the two sentences together with a comma. Such punctuation is too weak. A comma is used between three or more clauses in a series, or, sometimes, between independent clauses joined by *and, but, or,* and *nor.* The comma should not be used alone to join two sentences.

INCORRECT: My father and my brother dug the well, it took them three weeks.

REVISED: (Any of the revisions under Run-on Sentences.)

THE SHORT, THE LONG, AND THE MONOTONOUS.

There is nothing intrinsically wrong with either short or long sentences. However, monotony or a lack of sentence variety is a weakness rather than an error. Too many short sentences may produce writing that is choppy and hard to follow. Short sentences may seem too simple and child-like.

> WEAK PATTERN: I had a dog. He was a collie. I called him Ring. He had white fur around his neck. I got him when I was seven.
>
> REVISION: *When* I was seven, I got my first dog, a collie, which I named Ring *because* he had white fur around his neck.

On the other hand, too many long and involved sentences may be equally difficult for the reader to understand. The principle here is that the sentence length and structure should offer variety and proper emphasis as well as clarity.

Sentence length is one of the few areas in writing where speech patterns can be an aid in judging how and what to revise. Read your material aloud. See if the emphasis and pace seem right. If you find you have to make too many unnatural stops, the sentences may be too short and simple. If you find you run out of breath before you can finish reading your sentences, they may be too long. If, after a paragraph or so, each sentence seems to take about the same time to read, the pace and rhythm may be routine and monotonous.

If you are writing dialogue, however, the speech patterns of your subject should determine the shape of the sentences. If the speaker is very young or close-lipped, the sentences will be shorter and simpler than if the speaker is an adult or is given to rhetorical flourishes. And, in general, speech is simpler than written prose in its sentence patterns.

As a very loose guideline, in a quick survey of your prose, you should find few sentences under seven words in length and few over thirty words in length. The average will probably run between twelve and eighteen. For such revisions consider your purpose and your audience, and use your best judgment.

THE PRINCIPLE OF TOGETHERNESS.

Sentences are easier to read and understand when subjects are close to their verbs, when modifiers are close to the words they modify, and when word groups are not split or interrupted. Sometimes you can't satisfy all requirements simultaneously, but it is a principle to keep in mind as you give a final polish to your sentences.

WEAK: The old horse, despite his years of familiarity with the trail, tried to stubbornly cut through the underbrush to reach the corral which was snake-infested.

BETTER: Despite his years of familiarity with the trail, the old horse tried stubbornly to cut through the snake-infested underbrush to reach the corral.

Strengthening the Verbs

The stronger the verbs, the stronger the writing. That's a sound axiom, but, as with most advice about writing, it has to be used with sound judgment. In general, the following guidelines are valuable, but the principles can't be followed in all cases.

CHOOSING BETWEEN ACTIVE AND PASSIVE VOICE.

Active voice is preferable in the majority of statements because it preserves the basic actor/action pattern. Active voice is more direct, vigorous, and economical than passive voice.

ACTIVE VOICE: Josh slipped the plain gold band on Matilda's finger. (Emphasis on Josh as an actor. Nine words.)

PASSIVE VOICE: The plain gold band was slipped onto Matilda's finger by Josh. (Emphasis on gold band. Eleven words.)

Certain passive voice constructions can create problems with the placement of modifiers:

PASSIVE VOICE: With a red face and shaking hands, the plain gold band was slipped onto Matilda's finger by Josh. (Dangling modifier.)

AWKWARD: The plain gold band was slipped onto Matilda's finger by Josh with a red face and shaky hands.

Elimination of the passive voice also corrects the problem of placement for the modifier:

ACTIVE VOICE: With a red face and shaking hands, Josh slipped the plain gold band onto Matilda's finger.

To screen for the passive constructions in your writing, ask yourself, "Who is performing the action?" If you have written something like, "The horses were hitched to the wagon," then who did the hitching? Rewrite it as "Jake hitched the horses to the wagon." If you wrote, "The wagon was pulled by the horses," rewrite it as "The horses pulled the wagon." Converting from passive to active voice usually strengthens the prose.

WORD CHOICE.

In writing, *diction* refers to the selection of the best word to communicate a given idea. For a certain context and audience, a word or phrase may be too colloquial or too formal; it may be too vague, too obscure, too technical, too hip, or too old-fashioned. But word choice is more art than science. No one is perfect. And no one has all the answers.

Trust yourself. Trust your natural and traditional language patterns. *They may not be technically correct,* but minor flaws and colloquialisms best reflect the flavor of your experiences, your region, your family, and your "voice." Remember what I said in the previous chapter about my Indian friend who insisted on speaking in his own tongue? Trust who you are, and balance that against the conventions and abstract rules and guidelines of formal usage. Your readers want to know *you;* honesty and clarity are more important than correctness.

As you revise your manuscript, consider the following guidelines to improve your word choice:

1. Write naturally. Avoid stiff, formal, and pretentious phrasing. Don't write, "The traumatic injury to his left limb incapacitated him for six months." Say instead, "He broke his left arm and couldn't use it for six months."

2. Write directly and clearly. Avoid wordiness.

   WORDY: In the area of cooking I have always considered myself something of a failure.
   BETTER: I'm not a very good cook.

3. Write with a fresh voice. Avoid trite expressions, clichés, and well-used phrases.

   TOO FAMILIAR: I'm such a poor cook, I can't boil water.
   BETTER: I'm such a poor cook, I once put baking powder in the macaroni. It came out looking like sewer pipes.

4. Avoid overuse of terms that are hazy, vague, indefinite, or general, such as the following:

thing	type	some
aspect	instance	lot
situation	manner	strange
factor	bunch	tendency

5. Use familiar terms in preference to obscure, unusual, or technical words as long as there is no loss of clarity or precision. Provide definitions where they are necessary. For example, the word *lister*—a term for a special type of plow—might be the precise term you want to use, and in that case you should use it and define it. But if *plow* will say what you want, then use it instead, because it will be more familiar to the average reader. For terms like *singletree* or *whiffletree,* you have little choice but to use those terms and explain them for the reader.

6. Double-check the meaning and use of terms that sound like other words. The following pairs are only a few of those that are often troublesome:
   accept   except
   affect   effect
   allusion   illusion
   already   all ready
   bail   bale
   brake   break
   comtemptible   contemptuous
   luxuriant   luxurious
   sensory   sensuous   sensual

7. Use a dictionary and thesaurus when revising vocabulary and spelling.

SPELLING.

In one sense, spelling isn't important at all. If you write *chose* for *choose* it isn't going to destroy the communication. If you write *reciept* for *receipt,* your cousin won't catch it and your great-niece won't care. Approach spelling as a minor final problem in the revision process:

1) Read over your revised copy and use a dictionary to check the meaning and spelling of any difficult words.
2) If you believe that a review of spelling rules and guidelines and/or a glossary of "demon" words will reassure and assist you, then consult an appropriate handbook.
3) Ask others to check your spelling. The copy for this book has been checked and proofread by at least five different professionals before going to press.
4) Accentuate the positive—97.4 percent of what you've done is correct.

Guides and Guidelines

Even these few guidelines are not principles and rules to be memorized, nor are they a measure of the competence and quality of your writing. Your natural voice and style ought to survive any polishing. You want only to clean up a few smudges, not to render the whole work antiseptic.

Don't let grammar intimidate you, and don't let authoritarian rules intimidate you. I can't tell you how often I've heard friends and relatives say, "I feel self-conscious about writing letters to an English teacher. I just know what must be going through your mind." Such intimidation reaches pretty high up the ladder, because I've known college professors of history and engineering who get defensive about their spelling and punctuation. Even the media—print and broadcast—are chastised by over-zealous grammarians who lament every deviation from formal usage.

In the professional, academic, and commercial worlds, strict standards may be justified. After all, the "error," if indeed there is one, reaches an audience of millions. But for the writer of family history and personal memoirs, such carping on minor rules is unfortunate and unimportant. What is important is content, the communication of information about people and family life. Even flawed communication is better than no communication.

If you have a family member who offers any negative criticism about the style or correctness of your writing, do one of three things: (1) Ask if he or she wants to remain on your distribution list. (2) Say that you are looking forward to reading some of his or her material so you will have a good model to imitate. (3) Best of all, thank your local grammarian and say you have much need of a proofreader and would be delighted to submit future copy for correction before publication. That will free up your time and reduce inhibition. Then you can write more, which is what you and your audience really want, anyhow.

As a final disclaimer, let me say that this chapter is not a comprehensive health plan for ailing prose. At best it is a finger on the pulse. For peace of mind and a good night's sleep, take two books: a dictionary and a thesaurus. If the thesaurus causes dizziness, discontinue use. Handbooks may provide some relief, but prolonged use may result in lethargy, blurring of vision, and disorientation. Writer's block is best treated by writer's cramp. The best program for healthy prose is daily writing exercise.

x A Review of Principles

> Write. Knowledge, interesting experiences, good intentions, and the best advice in the world are useless unless you write.

The writer of family history and personal memoirs has several advantages over other writers. Not the least among those advantages is the deep personal interest and enthusiasm the family audience brings to the material. That interest and enthusiasm make a wide variety of otherwise routine topics meaningful and important. Average people take on special significance. Some remote homestead is more important than the history of nations. The simplest sentences unfolding the story of family life become great literature, to be cherished and honored. With each future generation the audience grows larger; the memories, the details, the observations, the dreams more heroic, mythic echoes in the landscape of time. A voice sounds down the generations. It all begins and ends with words on paper.

To summarize and review what has been said up to this

point, we go back to the basic premises, the context out of which we write. Those premises provide the orientation from which all else follows:

1. The medium: the written word. That may seem obvious, but many people experiment with substitutes—the photograph or movie film or videotape. But nothing is more efficient, more economical, more revealing, or more far-reaching than the written word. The past, lost moments, thoughts, and aspirations are revealed best through words. Some people would substitute the spoken word for the written word, and that is certainly better than nothing, especially if it is tape-recorded. But few of us speak with the same intimacy and fluency that we can develop in writing. The speaker has little option for contemplation or reflection. He or she has little time to *compose* and almost no chance to edit. The audience cannot alter the pace of the recorded voice; nor can the audience easily and quickly search out selected information as long as the voice remains in the recorded form. The recorded form is a bit more difficult to produce and reproduce, more expensive and more fragile. There is a place for taped statements during interviews, especially for those who are unwilling or unable to write. Eventually most taped material will find its way into the written form through the grace of some transcriber.

   Given the choice and the opportunity, write.

2. The audience: family and friends. They are the best of audiences; a small, immediate group in the present, perhaps thousands in the future. The family message is their message. Their self-concepts and their egos are tied up in those words. They are

sympathetic, tolerant, involved, and motivated—
and they become more so generation by generation.
No writer could ask for more.

3. The writer: author, authority, voice, creator. You.
You must answer the questions, "Who am I? What
shall I reveal, give form, send forth into the future
that it may help others know themselves? What is
more important than this?"

4. The message: mustard seed. Grains of sand. Drops
of water. Small. Tight. Compact. The edifice is built
brick by brick, stone by stone. Take the simple
things. Take short time periods. Take clearly
defined acts with clear beginnings and endings.
Look for the unities of time, place, action or object
or theme. Design and compose short essays and
profiles and narratives and descriptions. Keep it
short and simple.

   Work up a list of topics. Let every possible
thought and idea and memory and little thing have
its place. Let the list continue to grow. Have big
lists and little topics, not the other way around.

   Begin anywhere and write about the topics you
like and know best. Indulge yourself writing of
those people, places, things, and events that you
love or have loved, that created wonder, awe, mys-
tery, emotion—those things that make you what
you are—that make the family what it is . . . and
will be.

5. The way: write. Write a little each day, every day.
Write a natural, easy rough draft. Get the thoughts
and images on paper. Get it down.

   Write several pieces in rough-draft form until
the flow and habit become natural and familiar.

Revise, when and how it suits you.

Children are not easy, but they are worth it.

6. The process: start with a small topic; expand it from the inside. Open it up. Develop the message in depth. Provide details, examples, facts, information, statistics, evidence, and images. Provide sensory details—things seen, heard, felt, smelled, and tasted. Provide ninety percent information; ten percent opinion, evaluation, and interpretation. Use dialogue. Let the subject come alive. Remember that your future audience knows very little of the people and things you write about.

7. The finishing touches: revise. Solve the big problems first: Bring the topic under control; then the development; then the organization. Take on the work paragraph by paragraph, revising introduction, body, and conclusion so that each part does its appropriate job. Take on the sentences. Tighten them up. Take on the words. Proofread the finished copy.

8. The final product: the annual publication, a collection of five, ten, or fifteen short pieces; written, reproduced, and ready for distribution to the audience list by the *deadline*. Pick a due date and stick to it. On the calendar mark the delivery date, and then back up two or three weeks and mark the copying date, and a month before that the preparation of the finished copy, and two weeks before that the last piece and last revision. The ten months prior to that is the writing time, doing a little bit each day.

One of our early premises was that writing is no more difficult than most other life skills. But perhaps after reading forty thousand words on how to do it, it sounds complex and difficult. That's characteristic of almost any process: The doing is easier and quicker than the detailed analysis and explanation of what's going on. For example, try to explain everything that is happening to the driver and his automobile as she or he pulls out of a driveway: nerves signaling, senses feeding back, gasoline vaporizing, gears meshing. List and explain each plant in the garden, its life cycle, pests and diseases that attack it, planting, fertilizing, pruning. Make out a menu for a year, including types of food, methods of preparation, exact portions, temperatures, vitamin content, minerals. The result would be overwhelming. But, in fact, people drive and garden and cook without being inhibited by the underlying complexity of the task. Writing is the same way. You do it naturally if you do it as often as you drive or garden or cook. Occasionally you read a cookbook or a manual on roses to pick up a few pointers. You learn what you need, and you ignore the rest. Do the same here.

Postwriting

xi Organizing the Publication and Choosing Graphics

The writer must group the short pieces and make decisions about photographs and overall design.

This is composing on a different level. Where the writer puts together words, sentences, and paragraphs, the "editor" puts together articles and graphics. At this stage you design the annual magazine of family history that was mentioned in chapter II. If you are thinking in terms of a book rather than an annual publication such as a magazine, the information here still applies. Instead of designing a magazine, you are designing a chapter or subsection.

The Dummy

Your best friend is a dummy. It will save you time and money, and it will help you produce a finer quality publication.

The "dummy" is a *physical* outline or model for the annual magazine. Start with blank paper. Assuming the magazine pages will be standard 8½-by-11 white bond paper, make the dummy from the same size paper.

On the first sheet of paper write in bold letters, "Title Page." If you have a working title, pencil that in also, and add your name as author, your address and telephone number, and the words "Copyright 19xx."

Pick up a second sheet of paper. In the upper-right-hand corner number it, "page 2." At the top of the page write, "Dedication," and under that some parallel marks with the pencil to show where the text will go.

On the third sheet write, "page 3," and the words, "Table of Contents." If you know the sequence in which you are going to arrange your pieces, write down their titles in that sequence. If not, you can leave it blank until later. You won't know the actual page numbers until all the copy is finished in its final form.

On page 4 you might write, "Preface." In the space below, you might write some personal comments on your purpose, your philosophy, your reasons for writing on the subjects contained in this issue of the magazine, etc. You might also give credit to anyone who helped you.

The "Preface" might be continued on page 5.

On page 6 of my dummy, I would draw a horizontal line across the middle of the page dividing it into an upper and lower half. In the upper half I would draw an oval and sketch in a couple of stick figures and write the words, "Photograph of Maude and John Hofmann taken about 1905." In the bottom half I would draw another oval and three stick figures. Below that I would write, "Their three sons, Louis, Roy, and Howard, about 1910."

Page 7 of the dummy could say, "Summary of Grandpa's life."

Pages 8 and 9 would be, "Summary, cont'd," but at the bottom of page 9, I might put in a square and stick figure and indicate "Photo of Mary Hofmann about 1920, shortly before her death."

On page 10 I might use a photo of Grandpa and Grandma from a later date.

Pages 11 through 15 would be devoted to the piece, "Grandpa's Wooden Leg."

Page 18, photo, Grandpa in a bowler hat.

Pages 19 through 22, "The K. of C. Poker Party."

And so on. A photo here or there; a summary on Grandma's life; a sketch about Grandma; a piece on my father or me, until I had put together a facsimilie or dummy containing the stories and graphics for my annual magazine.

The dummy is a page-by-page outline of the publication as you conceive it. If you want to change something, make out a new page. If you want to change the sequence of the stories, shuffle the pages and renumber them. The dummy is a working device much like an outline to help you design a better product. Changes and mistakes and corrections are cheap and easy in a dummy. They are expensive and difficult in the final magazine.

The dummy will go through several changes and revisions. After you have read the next chapter on reproduction and costs, you may want to change the dummy again. When all the factors have been put into the formula, make out a final dummy. If you decide to run your copy back-to-back, that is, with words on both front and back of the pages, then staple or tape the dummy pages together, back to back. Move the left-hand page numbers to the outside, upper-left-hand corner of the page. Make a note to the typist to type the left-hand page numbers and the left-hand page margins to allow for the binding.

You should have your final dummy worked out before preparing the final copy of your manuscript and before contracting for reproduction. Take the dummy with you if you are talking to a typist, or if seeking bids for reproduction. Have the dummy available for whoever is doing the reproduction, collating, and binding.

Organizing the Magazine

Your five to ten pieces should be fairly easy to put in order. If you have written on a variety of small, simple topics on various themes and subjects, then you can gather them up as a bouquet and pass them along to your friends and relatives in almost any order. If you have sampled freely among your topics, touching on different times, themes, activities, and people, then almost any order will do.

However, if you think one or two pieces are clearly better than the others, then there is an advantage to starting with a good piece and ending with a good piece. If one or two pieces are sober or sad, put them in the middle. Start and end with lighter, gayer, or more uplifting topics. Alternate longer and shorter pieces. Look at the table of contents for the *Reader's Digest.* That magazine combines commentary, stories, biographical profiles, and personal experiences with an eye to variety. You can do the same in your magazine.

Some writers have talked to me about grouping material according to subject or theme, and that is fine. I have seen one collection of family writing in which fifteen or twenty different people wrote about their memories of a house that several generations had occupied or visited. The organization was loosely chronological, but several descriptive pieces and personal expressions could have been placed almost anywhere in the group.

Even if you wrote seven or eight pieces about one person, the organization of those pieces might still be very loose. Consider the two pieces about my grandfather— the one on his wooden leg and the other on his poker playing. They do not have to follow each other in any order. Neither piece is causally nor conditionally dependent on the other. It is true that the summary of his life should come first in such a collection, because it will provide a meaningful background for the pieces that follow. That should be your guiding rule for sequencing the different pieces: If one piece provides necessary background or context for another, place it first, but keep in mind that most of your pieces are self-contained and can stand alone.

On the other hand, if you are combining a tighter history of the family—how they moved from Boston to the wheat fields of Kansas and finally to the Willamette Valley in Oregon—then your final arrangement of the pieces should be chronological, following the year-by-year or decade-by-decade progression of moves and events. But I stress the *final* arrangement, because while you might put the pieces together in a certain order, *you don't have to write them in that order.* The first year you might combine pieces on the Boston home, the Kansas ranch, and the Oregon farm. The next year you might have a piece on the train ride from Boston to Kansas. The third year you might write about the stopover in Chicago or St. Louis and do a piece about the family's eighteen months in Salt Lake City before moving on to Oregon. Five years later all those pieces might be recombined into an expanded publication and put in a new chronological order.

The organization of the annual magazine can be seen as nothing more than an interim arrangement while the greater work goes on.

Using Photographs

As an amateur photographer and sometime cinematographer, I value photographs. I delight in each new studio portrait of my daughters and each new discovery from the family archives. But I know that the dozens of photographs I have of my grandfather say nothing about his wooden leg; nor do they communicate anything of the relationship he had with me or his wife or his sons or his daughters-in-law.

By the same standards I know that I could never render the face and physical presence of my grandfather as well as those few photographs do. Within their range photographs possess a phenomenal power.

The secret, then, is to capitalize on the strength of both media. Writing and graphics can be combined to complement each other. For example, character and personality and conduct can be exploited best in writing; but face and dress and physical world may be rendered best in a photograph. A way of life, such as the hardships on a dry-land homestead, can be made intense and poignant in writing, but a photograph of a board shack and tumbledown wagon may validate and confirm the prose. The right photograph has a way of making a story more real and immediate. Rightly or wrongly, we trust photographs. Their documentation seems unquestionable.

CHOOSING PHOTOGRAPHS.

What you want in the family writing and in the family photo are images that reveal. If I showed you a picture of my Uncle Irl (the beekeeper, the farmer, the builder of turkey blinds) in a suit, it would be misleading. He favored felt and straw hats, khaki shirts and riding breeches, and boots. For that reason snapshots often are more valuable than formal portraits in defining character. Look for photographs of people in their natural, daily environment. Look for photographs of people at work and at play. Look for the workaday, weekday image, not the Sunday best.

Use medium shots or close-ups in preference to wide-angle or panoramic shots. Just as in writing, the close-up reveals more details than does the broad overview. A picture of ten people in a group results in faces the size of peas. The best of landscapes turns to gray mush.

Whenever it is possible, use photographs with people

in them, even if the main subject is a building, an object, or a locale, because the human form gives us a sense of scale by which we can judge the size of buildings, equipment, and terrain.

Look for photographs that are close in time or theme to the subject you are writing about. I don't have any photographs of turkey blinds and wouldn't use them if I did, but I have several photographs of my uncle with a turkey in one hand and a shotgun in the other. That would be thematically suitable and more interesting for my readers than looking at a hole in the ground.

Look for photographs that are as clear and as revealing as possible. Favor images with good focus, good exposure, and good contrast. Faded and washed-out images will not reproduce well.

Black-and-white originals are better than color originals for reproduction. Cost makes color reproduction impractical for most budgets. That means that color originals must be converted to black-and-white copies. Color originals often fade or yellow out, and the images copied from them often lack contrast.

Larger-size originals produce better quality reproductions than do smaller ones. In all graphics reproduction it is better to start with large-size originals and reduce them to fit the page than with small-size originals and enlarge them to fit the page. If you have the photographic negative for a small 2-by-3 print, you will get better-quality reproduction if you have a new 5-by-7 print made from the negative.

In reality, it is almost impossible to have family photographs meet all the above conditions. Snapshots of people at work rarely are large size, with good contrast and sharp focus. Our most valued old photographs are invariably studio poses, and they are often faded or stained. In making your choices, use the best of what's available.

OTHER PICTORIAL IMAGES.

The family photo album may be the most obvious source of graphic materials, but it is not the only one. The large portraits on the wall, either photographs or paintings, can be photo-reduced in size to fit the format of the family history magazine. The same is true for a variety of other images.

Paintings, etchings, and drawings are quite suitable for the family history—expecially the latter two, which may reproduce directly on a photocopy machine. Such graphics may be family heirlooms or they may be current renderings. Some writers with artistic skills produce their own drawings and paintings to accompany their written text.

Museums, libraries, historical societies, and the like maintain archival holdings where old photographs, paintings, etchings, and prints (a view of the city in 1850) are available for copying. Period maps, newspaper reports, and a variety of documents may be available for copying.

From either family or private or public collections, writers might acquire photocopies of posters, flyers, maps, records, diplomas, certificates, licenses, or forms. It is often possible to obtain facsimiles of letters, pages from diaries or journals, or the family Bible, which might be included in the family history.

The possibilities here are endless: Consider blueprints or patent drawings, report cards or wedding invitations, children's art, office letterheads from the family business, mortgages, military orders and discharge certificates, sheet music, old receipts, and canceled checks.

Even three-dimensional objects, if they have enough relevance and significance, can be photographed for inclusion in the memoir or history. For example, a Civil War sword or uniform that is a one-of-a-kind item can be photographed and then reproduced in the family magazine. The same is true for unusual jewelry, watches, furniture, tools, needlework, and so on.

The only qualification is that the graphic image should support and enhance the written statement and/or provide special information to the reader.

Other Graphic Devices

There are all kinds of artwork, signs, and symbols that commercial magazines and other publications use constantly. Many of these come ready-made; there are sheets of art designs, illustrations, or symbols that can be purchased in art-supply stores. Most of this material is prepared for commercial artists and graphic designers in advertising, publishing, education, and public relations. If you want a drawing of a typical turn-of-the-century farm kitchen, it's out there waiting for you. If you want a sketch of a doughboy in World War I, it's there, right next to the marine-corps symbol and the logo for Ford Motor Cars.

Even more common are the hundreds of transfer letters used in the preparation of graphic copy. These ready-made transfer letters come in a variety of sizes and styles and can be used for the cover or title page of the publication if you're not satisfied with standard typeface. You can even carry them over to the title page of each story or article. But don't get carried away. Transfer letters, special graphic art, drawings, and photographs will add to the complexity of preparation and the cost of reproduction. Graphics are nice but not necessary. You've done your major work when you have finished the writing.

Combining Written and Graphic Elements

The selection and placement of the pictorial elements depend to a great extent upon the type of reproduction you use for the family magazine (see the following chapter). For reasons of cost and convenience, the majority of writers will choose either photocopy or offset printing or a combination of the two to make copies of the magazine. Therefore, the following guidelines apply primarily to copy being prepared for those reproduction media.

BASIC ARRANGEMENTS.

Make *a dummy* to work out the best combination of text and graphics. One of the simplest, cheapest, most effective ways of arranging illustrations in the magazine is already suggested in the description on preparing the dummy: Place a photograph or a pair of photographs on the page just before the title page of one or more of the pieces. Use the photograph to introduce your subject to the readers or to orient them to a time, place, or activity. Use the photo to set a theme.

Place a photo or an illustration at the end of the piece. If the written text ends near the top of the last page, consider inserting illustrative material across the bottom half of the page.

As a basic guideline, do not interrupt the text of your short pieces by inserting photographs or sketches in the middle of a page between paragraphs. Such placement distracts the reader, and it creates some problems in layout and reproduction. Keep it plain and simple unless you or some member of the family has special skills in graphic design and copy preparation.

Leave a generous one-and-one-half-inch border of white paper on each photo page. Don't expect the picture to extend to the very edges—those are called *bleed* edges, and printers can't print them without charging extra for trimming. Photocopy machines can reproduce full-page bleed images, but most pictures look better within a white margin frame.

Don't try to combine more than four photos per

page. Too many pictures mean small, undramatic images.

Don't cut up photographs to make a montage or mosaic or special shape. Original materials should be preserved intact, and montages are hard to label and harder to interpret.

Don't write on the photo image itself or draw circles or arrows to highlight specific features.

Type captions to be mounted on a strip below each photograph. Identify all subjects by full name, date, place, and occasion.

HANDLING PHOTOGRAPHS AND ORIGINAL ART.

The major concern is to preserve the quality and integrity of photographic and artistic materials. Treat one-of-a-kind items with respect, and take a few precautions:

1. Avoid getting fingerprints, even the cleanest ones, on photo surfaces. Handle photos carefully by the edges.
2. Don't leave photos or artwork in direct sunlight; the images will bleach and fade. Color is particularly susceptible.
3. Don't write on the backs of photographs with ball-point pens.
4. Do identify each subject by name, date, location, and occasion, and write your name, current address, and phone number, also, but *write or type on tape or labels specifically designed for use with photographic materials.* Affix those tapes or labels to the backs of prints or mounts. Don't use most transparent tapes; don't use water-base glues; don't use rubber cement.
5. Do use approved mounting materials when affixing photos to new backing. Check with your local photographic supply dealer for recommended mounting materials.

6. If you are sending material out to be rephotographed or copied, know whom you are dealing with. Don't send everything out at once. Send out a small job and wait until it returns. Check the quality of the copy and the quality of your original to make sure you will be satisfied entrusting the rest of your materials to that person or organization. If you have a lot of photographs or artwork to be processed, ask for competitive bids.

7. Don't plan to glue copies of pictures into your magazine unless you are printing only two or three copies. There's a cheaper, easier way. (See the following chapter on reproduction.)

SPECIAL CONSIDERATIONS.

Your photographs are likely to come in a variety of sizes. Some of them, the older ones, may be permanently mounted to heavy card stock. *Don't try to remove the photographs.* Have them copied on the mount.

A similar problem may exist with family albums. My aunt's old album had all the pictures glued in place with what seems to be mucilage. Someone tried to remove a few pictures—half of each picture is still there. If any photograph is glued down, leave it there.

Any photo or artwork larger than 8 by 10 inches must be reduced in size to fit a standard sheet of paper. A few rare photographs might have to be enlarged.

If you have the negative for a photograph, the cheapest route is to order a new print to your specifications and work with the new print.

If you don't have the negative, you must do one of the following:

1. Take the entire mount or album page to a photographer to have a copy made. The photographer should make a negative in the process, and you

should keep the new negative and new print. This approach is the most expensive, but the quality should be very good.

2. If you are dealing with an offset printer for the reproduction of the magazine (see the next chapter), entrust the printer to copy the original photo or artwork with a copy camera, making a screen negative from which he or she will make the plate for the press. The quality should be good and the overall cost moderate. Best of all, the printer will deliver fifty copies of the image at a price below what most commercial photographers would charge for one negative and print.

3. If you are willing to sacrifice a little quality, many of your graphics can be copied directly on the new photocopy machines that have the capability of reducing and enlarging images. For my purposes I find the quality acceptable, particularly if the original was of good quality. In small quantities of ten or so, photocopy is cheaper than offset, with some sacrifice in quality.

In a relatively short time everything will begin to pull together. In many ways the organization and design of the magazine is a much easier compositional problem than the original writing, but the mechanics and logistics of getting it printed may seem overwhelming. And you do have to watch the costs carefully. But if you work with the dummy, conceiving your final project in that trial-and-error fashion, adding, deleting, changing, and shuffling at will, you can do most of the design for your magazine in an afternoon or two. When you are satisfied with the design, make a final dummy, one page for each page in your magazine. Use it to help you along the final stages of copy preparation, layout, and reproduction.

After going through the process a time or two yourself, you'll be telling others how to do it.

xii Putting It All Together

The individual pieces become an annual magazine or a book.

Putting it all together means typing the final copy, adding any graphics, then reproducing, binding, and distributing the magazine or booklet.

Early in this book we stressed the principles of small, plain, and simple. Those principles should apply also to the final publication. Keep it simple. Every elaboration adds to the cost.

Cost is a major consideration in the advice and recommendations that follow, but any cost estimates are only rough approximations. Many variables such as inflation, regional price differences, size of the annual publication, number of photographs, type of binding will affect the final cost. In all cases you should make numerous inquiries to obtain the best possible prices for materials and reproduction services. Here are some basic recommendations:

1. Keep it simple.
2. Always work from a dummy design.
3. Always ask for bids from at least three sources.
4. Ask for quantity discounts.
5. Type the final manuscript copy.
6. Limit photos or other graphics to one or two per article. It is even cheaper to omit them altogether.
7. For 25 copies or less, photocopy is the easiest and cheapest method of reproduction. In the 25-to-50 copy range, photocopy is cheaper than offset printing for most projects. For 50 copies or more, offset printing quickly becomes the less expensive of the two processes and offers more options in graphic design.
8. For magazines of 100 pages or less, (a) staple copies with card-stock covers, or (b) bind in folio covers with clasp fasteners. Machine drill the holes for clasp or post binding.

Given current technology and pricing practices in my area, these recommendations provide for the best cost/quality balance for producing a magazine of family history or personal memoirs.

TYPING.

The final copy can be handwritten, but typing is preferable. Its uniformity is an advantage which outweighs the more "personal" handscript. Typing is clearer, easier to read, and more compact than most handscripts. (And that compactness can lower reproduction costs if it reduces the overall number of pages.) However, a handwritten manuscript is better than none.

There is always the chance that you can enlist someone else to do the typing. But if you don't type yourself and can't find a volunteer, you may have to pay someone. A professional will seem to cost more than an amateur, but the professional will probably be faster and neater. If the amateur bid isn't at least fifty percent less than the professional, go with the professional.

Bids may be by the hour, the job, or the page (so much per page of *finished copy*). Quotes by the job or by the page are more predictable. Avoid the open-ended hourly rate.

Prices quoted by professionals frequently include one or two copies with the original.

Proofread all copy and get corrections made before paying the full bill.

TYPING—MANUSCRIPT FORM.

It's possible to shave some cost here, but at a small sacrifice in readability. If you cheat on the recommended margins and use single space or space and a half instead of double space for the copy, you can cut your overall number of pages thirty to fifty percent, and cut the reproduction costs by almost the same percentages. However, what follows are guidelines for standard typed manuscript form. Any cost-saving deviations should be discussed with the typist. Show the typist your dummy and make sure that margins, pagination, spacing, and placement of copy are clearly understood and agreed upon *before* the work begins.

TYPEFACE.

The size of the type is not critical, but pica (the larger size) is preferred to elite. Standard typeface is much preferable to script, italic, all caps, or some of the ultra-modern styles. Go for the plain and simple rather than the fancy.

Typing should be done with a fresh ribbon and clean keys. Strike-overs should be avoided. Corrections can be made by erasing, or by using correction fluid or correction tapes. Type only on one side of the paper.

PAPER.

Standard 8½-by-11 inch plain white bond, twenty pound weight or better, is preferable for all copy. Treated bond with its easy-erasing finish is a problem: Some treated bonds smear, and their weight and texture sometimes cause jamming in auto-feed copiers. By all means, avoid onion skin and similar thin, light papers for your original. Good copies come from dark, sharp type on dense white paper.

SPACING AND MARGINS.

Standard form calls for double-spaced copy. Space and a half is still readable. Single space is a strain. If in doubt, ask the typist to give you three sample paragraphs with different spacing and judge for yourself.

The first page of each piece should begin with the title centered about four inches from the top of the page. Leave four spaces and begin the text.

The left-hand margin, because of the binding, should be one and one-half inches wide. Leave one-inch margins on the right and at the bottom. On all pages after the title page, begin the top line about one and one-quarter inch down. Other margins are the same as those on the title page, *unless you decide to reproduce the copy back-to-back. Then the binding margin on left-hand (even-numbered) pages are reversed: The one and one-half margin is on the right.*

PAGE NUMBERS.

Page numbers should go in the upper-right-hand corner, one-half inch down, one inch in from the right edge of the paper. The conventional guidelines say number each page consecutively, although the number may be omitted from the title page (it is still counted). But for the personal memoir or family history built up from small units, it might be preferable to number each story, essay, or vignette separately. That can be done by using a key word from the title followed by the page number, for example, *Turkey Blind—2* or *Wooden Leg—5.* If you believe you might recombine the pieces at a later time, such pagination might be desirable. For the family audience, either system is acceptable. Use the dummy as a page numbering guide.

Your typed copy will be your *original* or *master.* It should be kept neat and clean, and it should be stored carefully. For protection against loss or damage, keep a duplicate stored in some other location or residence. Neither the original nor the stored duplicate should be passed around for reading. Distribute only expendable reproductions.

Preparation of Copy for Reproduction

Your typed original is your reproduction master. Proofread it one last time.

If you want the cover, title, title page, or any story titles to have special lettering such as the rub-on transfer types, those should be applied now.

Any line art such as ink drawings or ready-made commercial art can be attached to the pages in their appropriate locations *if they are to scale*—that is, if they are the right size for reproduction.

NOTE: Sheets of paper with transfer letters, paste-up art, tape, and the like cannot be run through auto-feed mechanisms on photocopiers. Have a duplicate page made and inserted into the master copy.

Keep all photographs and oversize art separate. Don't intermix photo pages with the typed master just yet. Your dummy shows how everything will go together. Combine photographic materials and other special artwork with the master text *only after you have consulted with the copy or reproduction center to determine their preferred working format.* Take your final dummy along and let it speak for you.

Reproduction: Photocopy or Offset Printing

Whether you have a handwritten manuscript or a typed master, the problem is how to reproduce it for distribution to your audience at the best cost/quality ratio. From this discussion I have excluded such options as the carbon master or spirit master, which produce the purple-toned "ditto" copies. Such reproduction is cheap, but the copies have only fair legibility and the print fades, especially when it is exposed to sunlight. Stencil masters that produce "mimeograph" copies are more difficult to type, but the copy is readable and permanent. For those with access to mimeo equipment, that system might provide a slight cost advantage. However, the system is not as widely available as photocopy or offset printing, which are the two systems capable of providing the best cost/quality ratio.

CHOOSING BETWEEN PHOTOCOPY AND OFFSET.

Quantity is a key factor in the cost of reproduction. The greater the number of pages per magazine, the greater the cost. But the greater the number of magazines, *the lower the cost per unit.* You can run ten copies of a fifty-page magazine for twenty to fifty dollars on photocopy machines. Ten copies of a fifty-page magazine on an offset press (an impractical quantity) would cost a hundred dollars. But fifty copies on offset would cost the same hundred dollars. If you could justify thousands of copies, the per-unit cost on an offset run would drop fifty to seventy percent or more.

For that reason each writer should give close and careful consideration to the size of his or her distribution list. Where audience size warrants it, quantity orders can result in significant per-unit savings. For our purposes we will assume a family magazine with fifty pages of typed manuscript and a few photographs. The number of magazines printed—the quantity run—will vary.

In quantities of twenty-five or less, photocopy is cheaper, and the quality on new machines is excellent; but don't expect cheap prices or the best quality from a do-it-yourself coin-operated machine in your local drugstore or supermarket. The best machines, the best service, the best quality, and the best prices can be had from professional copy or reproduction centers. They will save you time and a lot of quarters.

When you approach any copy service, always ask for quantity discount prices. In quantities of twenty-five to fifty, the cheapest photocopy price is less than the cheapest offset. But technology is producing rapid changes. Many reproduction centers in my area offer the same cost figures on photocopy and offset in the fifty-to-one-hundred-copy range. *Each writer should determine cost advantages by seeking competitive bids from local sources.*

For the reproduction of typed copy, quality is equally good from either photocopy machines or offset presses. Until recently this wasn't true, but the modern photocopy machines in use in most copy centers use standard bond papers and provide excellent dark and uniform typeface reproduction. In some cases the copy machines produce better images than those on the original.

Both photocopy and offset can print pages back-to-back, but there is no real cost advantage to this practice in small runs of a fifty-page magazine. However, there are some esthetic advantages: The text is less bulky, and it looks more professional. On the negative side, it requires more careful attention to margins and pagination to avoid errors.

In terms of overall options offset has the advantage, but if you are keeping the magazine project simple, those options aren't likely to mean much. High-speed presses, multicolor inks, special papers, and the like aren't options of much value given the economics of a family magazine.

In addition, you have to know more about design and layout to utilize those options.

But one option is critical: half-tone reproduction, the ability to reproduce photographic images. Offset presses provide better-quality reproduction of photographs than can be obtained on existing photocopy machines. However, in this area there is a real tradeoff in choices. If you want lots of photographs in your family magazine and can sacrifice a little on quality, photocopy remains the cheaper alternative for small runs.

Either system, photocopy or offset, will be slightly inferior to good-quality original photographs. However, both systems may actually improve the quality of faded originals. To make your own choice on photographic reproduction, reproduce one or two photographs on the best photocopy machine at a copy center. If you are satisfied with the photocopy image, then use that process, because it is cheaper than any other generally available process in quantities under two hundred copies. Good-quality offset should be equal to the black-and-white images in most slick magazines.

Some photocopy machines can also enlarge or reduce the size of photographs. Quality may suffer. Make a few test runs. Offset cameras offer a wider range of enlargements and reductions and can work with much larger originals, such as paintings, than photocopy machines can handle. Offset cameras produce little loss in quality, but labor and materials costs make the end product more expensive than photocopies in quantities under two hundred units.

Both systems are much cheaper than having copies made at a photographic studio, and there is no mounting or paste-up of individual magazine pages.

NOTE: The exposure to intense light in photocopy machines may cause fading or fogging in some photographic originals.

Final Steps

After reproduction of copies a few mechanical chores remain.

COLLATING.

Collating refers to the gathering and assembling of the loose copy pages in the correct order for binding. Collating is often done automatically without extra charge to a customer, but the writer should make a specific inquiry about the service when contracting for reproduction. If an extra fee is charged for collating, the writer can consider doing the job, especially if the number of issues is small.

BINDING AND COVERS.

For the family magazine, only a few binding options are economically feasible:

Stapling. Fifty pages are too much for most hand staplers. Reproduction centers have power staplers for materials of different thicknesses. The center may charge a minimal fee for the service but may provide it free or at a reduced rate if they also do the reproduction and collating.

Staple-bound magazines can have a cover sheet made from standard copy paper or from a flexible card stock cover. Words and/or designs can be reproduced on the card stock either by photocopy or offset processes. Since card stock comes in a variety of colors, this is one area where color can be introduced for relatively little increase in cost.

Cover stock, which is stiffer and more expensive than card stock, offers a wider range of colors, textures, and finishes.

Clasp and ring binders. There are many types of these

wraparound folders and binders on the market. They offer good protection for the printed copy, stand up well under use, and are attractive.

The simplest and cheapest of these binders are the folders students use for writing projects. They are called folio or pocket-folio binders. Most of them have three metal prongs or clasps that pass through holes in the copy pages to hold the sheets in the folders. They have soft, sturdy covers and come in white, buff, and colors. Inquire about the varieties available at the reproduction center, a stationery store, an art-supply center, or a college bookstore. When you decide on what to buy, ask for a quantity discount.

For small runs of ten to twenty magazines, folios are probably the cheapest binding available.

More expensive are the rigid pressboard covers with metal or plastic clasps. They are two to five times as expensive as the folio covers, but they are also more durable and attractive and will hold more pages—up to three hundred sheets. You might use two or three of these for special presentations and the cheaper ones for general distribution.

Probably the most familiar is the old loose-leaf ring binder, but if you haven't priced one lately, the cost will shock you. They can be purchased in small sizes that will hold fifty to one hundred pages, but there are a lot of problems with sheets tearing loose from the binding posts. From a cost and utility perspective, they are less suitable than folio or pressboard binders.

Drilling. For all clasp and ring binders, it is necessary to drill or punch holes in the binding margin of the magazine. Even for the stapled bindings, which may find their way into other covers or folders, drilling is a good idea. Most reproduction centers can drill the sheets a ream at a time, and it's worth the nominal cost for the quantities we're discussing. Hand-operated gang punches are a possible do-it-yourself substitute, but only as an act of penance.

Spiral and comb bindings.   You have seen these around. Steno note pads and special writing tablets have wire spiral bindings. The plastic comb binding is similar, but the teeth are flat, parallel strips that hook into custompunched rectangular holes. Bindery charges for a small job are too high for most budgets, but comb and spiral bindings are competitive in price with ring binders. However, the service is not available in all communities, and the bound sheets are permanently set, whereas other folders and binders permit insertion and deletion of individual pages.

Stitched and/or glued bindings.   Widely used commercially, these binding techniques are not readily available in most communities, and many binderies cannot take on small jobs at a reasonable cost. However, if you are talking about an extensive manuscript of several hundred pages and/or a run of several hundred copies, this may be the best option. I have seen family projects bound in this fashion when the magazine was issued in a hundred copies. Obtain several bids for any job of this type.

One remote possibility in this area is to use the binding service at some libraries, colleges, universities, and private institutions. You might be able to strike a deal with a library, museum, or college whereby they would bind a limited number of books in return for a donation of your manuscript to their collection. If your material has historical and/or literary value, you might be in a good bargaining position.

Fund Raising—Sharing the Load

If you can't afford it, there is no reason you should bear all the costs for typing, reproducing, and binding the magazine. Even if you can afford it, involving other members of the family in the project helps draw everyone closer together. Here are some possibilities:

1. Make it a group project from the start, with two, three, or more persons sharing the writing, design, and costs.
2. Solicit services. See if someone in the family can do the typing or work on graphics or arrange to have the copying done at reduced cost. Use a family member to help with collating and/or binding operations.
3. Solicit funds. Ask family members to contribute cash to defray expenses, either partially or totally.
4. Solicit funds. Look for a patron. Many people who are sincerely interested in the family history would rather offer financial support than have to do the writing.
5. Solicit funds and/or services from state and local governments, foundations, libraries, special collections, historical societies, etc. Start with your local librarian and ask about grants and other funding options. Check with historical societies on the local and state level—their number is increasing, and they may help raise funds. Remember, your writing is history, a type of historical writing that is now in its ascendancy.
6. Substitute costs. Make the magazine your Christmas or birthday gift to various families, family members, and friends. There couldn't be a better homemade gift, and the money you would have spent on ties, pot holders, and vases now goes toward a worthwhile and cherished gift. For those members of the family who should be doing their own writing, buy them a copy of this book.

7. Transfer funds. Tell your relatives and friends you'd rather have money for your project than ties and pot holders for Christmas or your birthday.

When you're stumped halfway through a paragraph or when you're in the middle of reproduction hassles, you may not believe it, but it's worth it. When you receive the gratitude and compliments of family and friends, you'll know it's worth it. When you see last year's copy jammed among the outdated magazines beneath the end table, you may suffer pangs of doubt, but as the copies accumulate over the years and their status and quality grow, so will your confidence in the certainty that it was worth it. Inside yourself, with the rediscovery of each memory, face, and event you examined in the hours of writing, there is never any doubt.

xiii Second Thoughts: Commercial Publication

Publication of the memoirs and family history by commercial houses for the mass market has not been part of the operating premise behind the guidelines in this book. But the question invariably arises.

Praise and publication are not synonymous. The friends and relatives who are sympathetic toward you and often personally involved with your material are not objective critics and are not the same as a paying audience. The fact that they like what you have written does not mean the general public will. Publishing is a money-making activity—or it hopes to be—and publishers must judge material not on its literary merits or on its worthiness but, rather, on its ability to make a profit.

Among the people I have worked with on memoirs and family history, a few have been able to place short pieces in regional magazines, and one or two have placed short pieces in small national magazines. Few have tried and none have succeeded in placing a book manuscript with a reputable publishing firm.

If some publisher offers to publish your work but insists that you help share the costs until the profits start coming in, get a lawyer. Such offers are legitimate, but the implied promises are often misleading; the publisher may know that there will never be any profits from the sale of the book. The company will get its profits from your subsidy of the printing costs.

Subsidy publishing—the author paying to have his or her book published—is a world away from the modest ten-to-fifty-copy reproduction for family and friends we have been talking about. Subsidy publishing for a book requires a formal contract filled with legal language, and big money up front: five to ten thousand dollars and more. It involves promotion, publicity, distribution, warehousing, and a lot more. Don't enter such a venture without first consulting three of your immediate relatives, two lawyers (one of whom should be familiar with the publishing world), your banker, and a nonsubsidy publisher and/or an agent. If they agree that your book is marketable and the gamble is worth it, ask them to put up the money and share in your profits.

Similar precautions should be taken with any individual or organization asking for money in return for appraising, editing, publishing, promoting, or distributing your work. I have appraised and edited manuscripts for a fee, and I assume that the writers got their money's worth. It's a legitimate service, but be leery of the sixty dollars appraisal that is very complimentary but suggests editing or rewriting that costs five thousand dollars, followed in six months by a request for another seventy-five hundred dollars to "begin" publication, and then another bite and another bite. Someone who is willing to work for a percentage interest in your manuscript is sharing the gamble; someone who is always asking for money has got a sucker on the line.

In the world of subsidy publishing, few writers break

even and fewer still ever make money on books they've paid to publish. But it does happen, and that's what makes for gold rushes, bingo, and blind dates.

In Search of Publication

If you go looking for a publisher, you have embarked on a different adventure from the family magazine we have been discussing. A new set of rules, guidelines, and standards applies. Some of the advice in this book is contrary to the guidelines for preparing material for commercial publication.

There are hundreds of books on the market that will tell you how to write for publication and how to find a publisher. Ask your local librarian for help, but on your own you can consult some of the following works:

1. *Writer's Market.* Cincinnati: Writer's Digest. Annual. That publication lists not only regional, national, and specialty markets but also agents, literary services, contests and awards, writers' clubs, writers' conferences, and writers' organizations nationwide.
2. *The Writer's Handbook* by A. S. Burack. Boston: The Writer, Inc., 1981. Similar to *Writer's Market* but offers more chapters on instruction and less information on markets.
3. *The Literary Market Place.* New York and London: R. R. Bowker Co. Annual. A business directory of book and magazine publishers. It also includes names and addresses of literary agents, writers' associations, etc.
4. If you are looking for publications in a certain state, province, or city, consult *Ayer Directory of Publications and Newspapers,* Philadelphia: Ayer Press. Annual.
5. The Coordinating Council of Literary Magazines,

80 Eighth Avenue, New York, New York 10011, publishes a *Catalog of Literary Magazines.* Many of these "little magazines" have circulations of under a thousand copies, and they usually do not pay for their material, but they are legitimate and important outlets for writers of nonfiction, fiction, poetry, drama, and a variety of mixed media and visual forms.

6. The most common periodicals for the writer in search of both markets and writing advice are *The Writer,* 8 Arlington St., Boston, MA 02116, and the *Writer's Digest,* 9933 Alliance Rd., Cincinnati, OH 45242.

Contact the writers' clubs and organizations in your area. They frequently conduct conferences and/or workshops at which you can pick up some valuable pointers on playing the publishing game.

Inquire at local high schools, community colleges, colleges, universities, community centers, YM/YWCAs, and the like about writing courses aimed specifically at publication. Many of the so-called creative writing classes won't deal with marketing principles and practices. Ask.

Freelancing the Book

Freelancing means you're on your own. Successful freelancers of nonfiction write book proposals before they ever write a book. It's more economical in terms of time and money, both for the writer and the editor. For that reason most handbooks on freelance writing suggest the following:

1. Do an outline and sample chapter, and submit them. If it interests an editor, he or she will ask for more.

2. Try to get a few short selections from the book published in some magazine, newspaper, or journal. If a magazine editor won't risk printing 1,000 of your words, why should a book publisher risk money on 100,000 of your words?

But that's only the beginning. Consult handbooks and articles for more definitive statements on the strategies and procedures of proposal writing.

Freelancing the Article or Biographical Sketch

This is one of the best ways to test-market your topics and writing skills.

1. Read up on the subject.
2. Start with your best material. Decide which magazines publish similar material. Everyone would like to score with the *Reader's Digest* and its audience of millions, but local and regional newspapers and magazines are the most likely candidates. They are a bit like your relatives and friends; they have an interest in you as a local personality and in your subject as local material.
3. Don't expect to get rich from your royalties. Some of the most likely publications won't pay anything; others will pay modest fees. Most will let you retain your copyright; others won't.
4. Everyone expects you to submit typed copy in proper format and to enclose a self-addressed stamped envelope (SASE) so the publication can return the material to you and give a reaction to it. That's about the only way you'll ever hear anything.
5. Mail out a high-quality photocopy of your manu-

script and keep your original. Keep a log sheet of what was sent to whom.

6. Response takes from two weeks to two months. After three months, inquire.

Copyright

There is a common fear among beginning writers that someone will steal their copyright. It's not a very reasonable fear. Historical events and literary ideas don't have much copyright protection. Your specific *composition* does have protection—enough so that it's cheaper for most publishers to pay you than to litigate with you.

On the title page of your magazine or article, put the words: *Copyright XXXX* (the year), *by XXXXXX X. XXXXXX* (your name), *XXXXXX* (city), *XXXXXXX* (state), and your address, if you want. Below the copyright notice add the words, *All rights reserved.* That should give you full protection of the law. It may not be worth much to you financially, but you'll sleep better.

Different publications have different policies about which copyrights they buy. You can sell part of your copyrights, such as the first North American serial rights, one-time publication in a North American periodical. That's slicing it about as thin as you can. That let's you keep second and subsequent serial rights, book rights, condensed-version rights, film rights, foreign rights, and so on.

Don't sign a "work for hire" agreement with a publisher unless you want to surrender *all* copyrights. A few publishers mail those "work for hire" agreements with every nickle-and-dime offer they make. Hungry authors and authors hungry for publication sign them.

Smaller publications sometimes don't even bother copyrighting their own material. In such cases tell the publisher you want to retain copyright and that you want a notice of copyright on the title page or lead of your article when it is published.

Copyright law changes, and no advice will apply uniformly in all copyright situations. Basic information on copyright can be obtained from:

Copyright Office
Library of Congress
Washington, D.C. 20559

Beyond that, consult a lawyer, preferably one who specializes in copyright law.

In general, you can avoid a lot of wasted effort and disappointment by sending your carefully chosen and carefully edited material to the appropriate magazine or journal. But don't be surprised if interesting and well-written pieces are rejected. An editor has to feel that your material is right for her or his readership, and the editor has to need it. Good material gets returned when an editor has too big a backlog or inventory of similar pieces.

Don't be surprised if you have to send a piece out five, ten, or fifteen times before it finds a home. You won't be breaking any records if you send a piece out forty or fifty times. I recently sold a piece that had been kicking around for fifteen years—I think the editor who bought it was still in high school when I wrote it.

But above all, don't take the responses of the commercial market too seriously. It's one thing to play around trying to get a few pieces published. It's another to lose sight of the goals and objectives we've been talking about throughout this book. Rejections from the commercial market say nothing about the value of your manuscript within your family structure. Commercial publication is an ephemeral thing. The best of prose is quickly shredded, burned, or composted. But the family history and the memoirs and the personal reminiscences lie quietly in the bosom of the family consciousness. Such writing will be taken out over the years and read and reread. With each generation the audience grows larger and the writing more valued.

Postscript

xiv From One Writer to Another

Since it is not granted us to live long, let us transmit to posterity some memorial that we have at least lived.

—Pliny the Younger, A.D. 62–113

Each of us stands at the apex of a pyramid of life. Supporting us are the two people who gave us birth—our parents—and supporting them, four people—their parents—and supporting them, eight and then sixteen. In a simple mathematical progression, if we go back fifteen generations, say to the sixteenth century, there are 32,768 lives merging to bring each of us into being. Our spouses bring a similar lineage, and our children look back to the sixteenth century where more than 65,000 lives constitute their heritage.

But in all probability, long before the sixteenth century we would find duplication, a common ancestral figure. And then another and another. In fact, our pyramidal structures share a common base confirming our brotherhood. In each of us merge king and pauper, saint and sinner, and thousands more.

We are also at the apex of another pyramid of life, this one unfolding into the future. Its lines and geometry are less distinct and certain than those of the past, yet it is to that multitude we write. Our words, like ourselves, are launched out of certainty and into uncertainty. But our words, like ourselves, help give shape to that uncertainty, direct it and confirm it, until others look back on it and wonder at the smooth patterns of its advance.

The genealogist looks back to establish what has been, but the writer of family history looks back only to glean the materials that will be composed in the present and transmitted to the future. From that perspective the family historian is a futurist—and an optimist.

The family historian is also a humanist in the best sense of that word, because he or she writes about the most human of events, the lives of men and women—not so much in the grand sweep of history or in the abstractions of politics, sociology, or psychology, but in the routine of daily living, in the labors and loves, in the joys and tears of individual human existence: the mother at work and in repose, the brother at play, the sister at prayer, the father at some task or hobby, the family together in the evening light.

The personal memoir or family history is a special kind of literature. There are writings of greater imagination and grander prose filled with heroes and heroines, myths and legends, the excitement of adventure and the throb of drama. Their prose rings. They sing, and we are enchanted. But the family history is made of more common stuff. Those humble words, like the earth, prevail and nourish and abide in the close-kept reaches of the individual spirit who reads them and says, "From this I come."

But if there were not an audience, and if there were no future, there would still be reason enough to write; for in writing we learn. Perhaps the function of all experience is for us to understand ourselves better, to reconcile the mysteries of body and soul. Certainly in the act of writing we come to understand our subject as we examine it and give it form. In so doing we shape ourselves, our attitudes, our insights, and our sympathies. The act of composition goes beyond the ordering of words to the ordering of mind. Memory is given discipline and purpose. Feelings are given form and voice. Perception and sensation are charged into new images. It is a mystical, almost a religious act, this examination of conscience, this confession. There is penance in the act itself, absolution as the task is done. There is cleansing as well as learning, and a purging as new grace flows in.

There occurs in writing like this a communion of past, present, and future that transcends our physical selves. Experience, thought, and feeling, once they are translated into words, survive. Through our writing we may put to rest old animosities, calm old tempests, soothe old wounds, relive old joys, renew old loves; pay homage, honor, cherish, and preserve. Whatsoever we preserve, preserves us.